The Incomplete Shakespeare

Hamlet

Annotated by
JOHN CRACE **JOHN SUTHERLAND**

Doubleday

LONDON · TORONTO · SYDNEY · AUCKLAND · JOHANNESBURG

HAMLET

Paul

Happy 65ᵗʰ birthday

with best wishes

John Cleese

DRAMATIS PERSONAE

OLD HAMLET	king of Denmark for thirty years
YOUNG HAMLET	king of Denmark for thirty seconds
CLAUDIUS	king of Denmark for five months (max)
FORTINBRAS	Norwegian king of Denmark for who knows how long
GERTRUDE	wife to any king of Denmark currently available
HORATIO	Hamlet's best friend from Wittenberg
ROSENCRANTZ AND GUILDENSTERN	no longer Hamlet's best friends from Wittenberg
POLONIUS	Claudius's Lord Chamberlain
LAERTES	Polonius's son
OPHELIA	Polonius's wronged daughter
OSRIC	dandyish man about the court, crooked as a three-ducat piece
THE REST	various 'men' (hirelings), 'players' (actors) and sundries, including a captain and kettledrum players.

1   Elsinore? Denmark? Why this interest by the country's leading playwright in Jacobean Scandi? It's explicable given the historical background in England in 1600–1601, when the play is presumed to have been first performed. The future James I had married a princess of Denmark, Anne, in 1589. She became an energetic queen of England, a lover of plays and a patron of the arts – Shakespeare's troupe is known to have played to her as guest of honour. Shakespeare was something of a king-pleaser. Very wise, given what happened to those who displeased the monarch.

2   Typical Danish names. Shakespeare's depiction of the country is a little economical. But he had done some homework. Elsinore is an anglicisation of Helsingør (which would not trip lightly off the tongue of an English actor). Situated strategically on Zealand, Elsinore guarded sea-trade routes – a main source of the conflict between Denmark and Norway which is central to the play. There was a magnificent, heavily fortified castle there where the Danish king often held court. He had a number of royal palaces at his disposal – this is something of an outpost. Why has Claudius chosen to be crowned here rather than in his capital, Copenhagen? The answer will emerge – he is not sure how the Danish people will react to the unusual circumstances in which he has come to the throne. He is an able but unloved monarch – unlike his predecessor, Old Hamlet.

3   It's an opening scene with a purpose. As will soon become clear, the court is celebrating a wedding. Why this armed guard and jumpy nervousness? High tension twangs like an overwound lute string.

4   Not an obvious choice of password, one might think. But, shouted out by Barnardo, it will resonate throughout the play. Kings, as it happens, don't live long in Elsinore. Three of them come to an untimely end during the course of the play. A record regicide score in Shakespeare's drama.

ACT 1, SCENE 1

The battlements of Elsinore castle[1]

Enter Barnardo and Francisco[2]

BARNARDO
Who's there?[3]

FRANCISCO
It's me.

BARNARDO
I know it is. But you're meant to use the password.

FRANCISCO
What password?

BARNARDO
'Long live the king.'[4]

FRANCISCO
Why didn't you say so earlier?

5   *Midnight. Bitterly cold, we're told more than once.
Shakespeare wants the audience to register the ominous fact
that it is the 'witching hour'.*

6   *The names are in order of precedence. Horatio, as etiquette
requires, is welcomed first, with a bow.*

7   *He can't bring himself to say the dreaded 'g' word. The midnight
watch will not have been popular in the guardroom over the
last few nights, with thingies hanging round the battlements.*

8   *Horatio, in addition to being the hero's best friend, is also by
nature a stoic (unexcitable) and a sceptic, philosophies we know
were taught at Wittenberg. His background is not revealed,
other than that he was present at Old Hamlet's battle against
Norway thirty years ago (!) and is also a fellow student of Young
Hamlet on Wittenberg campus. He is trusted by Claudius and
Gertrude, but he is also Hamlet's best friend and confidant. He
has been around for months, but Hamlet has not yet seen him
(what kind of best friend is that?). Shakespeare wins no prizes
for consistency on such trifling matters.*

9   *The earlier references to the 'bitter' cold establish this is winter,
when this northern area of Denmark is noir indeed. In a theatre
open to the elements, as the Globe was, weather matters, and is
often referred to by Shakespeare.*

BARNARDO
'Tis now struck twelve, so get thee off to bed,
Leave me to freeze my nuts off on these walls.[5]

Exit Francisco

BARNARDO
I hear a noise. What people this way come?

Enter Horatio and Marcellus

BARNARDO
Welcome, Horatio; welcome, good Marcellus.[6]

MARCELLUS
What, has this thing appeared again tonight?[7]

BARNARDO
I have seen nothing.

MARCELLUS
Horatio says 'tis but our fantasy,
And so I've brought him to these wretched steps
So he can witness it with his own eyes.[8]

HORATIO
I merely said you both spend too much time
Watching *The Bridge* and other Scandi *noir*.[9]

Enter ghost

10   *The ghost is 'it', not 'he'.*

11   *What they call the tone of command. 'Thou' is disrespectful.*
     Ghosts, ghostlore had it, only spoke if spoken to. Horatio
     – sceptic that he is – does not believe 'it' is the king, or his
     wraith, but a demonic imposter. Horatio, it is made clear,
     knew Old Hamlet personally. Legend has it that Shakespeare
     himself played the part of Old Hamlet. He's wearing armour,
     which establishes that, unlike Claudius, he is/was a warrior
     king. An old-school monarch, unlike his successor. The word
     'usurp'st' echoes meaningfully – a throne has been usurped,
     stolen. That point will be made over and again.

12   *Marcellus can always be relied on for a stupid remark.*

13   *War is smouldering on the edge of the play's action*
     throughout. Constant friction was breaking out in the area
     historically. Scandinavia (now Denmark, Norway and Sweden)
     had no defensible borders. The region is a powder keg.

MARCELLUS

Enough of that. Look where it comes again.[10]

BARNARDO

'Tis a dead ringer for our dear dead king.

HORATIO

What art thou that usurp'st this time of night,
In the same armour our late king did wear?
Stay! Speak, speak! I charge thee, speak![11]

Exit ghost

MARCELLUS

The ghost hath gone and answer made it none.[12]

HORATIO

That much I hath seen clearly for myself,
There is no need to state the obvious.
Since it did wear the very same armour
In which our good king Hamlet fought Norway,
Then surely Denmark must be in the mire.[13]

MARCELLUS

Since you're the brains, I'll put my trust in you
To tell me why a ghost foretells such doom.

HORATIO

'Tis time to fill thee in on our history:
When Hamlet killed Norway's King Fortinbras,

14   *The name Hamlet had a poignant resonance for Shakespeare. He had a son called Hamneth, or Hamlet (both forms are recorded), his only male child, in 1585. Young Hamlet died (of the bubonic plague then sweeping the country, it's presumed) in February 1596. His twin, Judith, survived. Shakespeare would have still been grieving while writing* Hamlet *(1599-ish, again it's presumed). Critics and biographers have plausibly found an elegiac tone in the play.*

     Fortinbras, the other princely son with the same name as his father, means 'strong in arm'. Formidable. Both Fortinbrases are always at the head of an army. Young Hamlet, unlike his armoured dad, routinely has his nose in a book. Old King Fortinbras fought Old King Hamlet, man to man. Old Hamlet won. Young Fortinbras, even after all these years, wants revenge. The newly crowned king of Denmark, Claudius, is more the wily diplomat: a ruler of the present, not the barbarous past.

15   *Yes – but here there may be another explanation. A whiff of incense wafts across this scene – see notes 37 and 50 on the subject of purgatory and 'Christian' ghosts.*

16   *Horatio is treading on very thin ice here. James I believed in ghosts, and gave specific instructions to his loyal subjects about how they should treat spectres. Disobeying this royal command would be unwise. A subsequent accusation of witchcraft or wizardry could cost you your life. James was passionate about killing witches.*

17   *It's winter in Denmark. Long, chill nights. But a minute or two ago, we recall, it was midnight. The clock chimed twelve. Now the cock crows – the traditional signal for ghosts and things that go bump in the night to be gone. Dawn would be late at this time of year in the northern hemisphere, around 9am or later. We are to assume that what we have witnessed – in 'jump' tempo – is a whole night on the battlements.*

Young Fortinbras did swear to vengeance take
And reclaim Denmark for his father's sake.[14]

MARCELLUS
So you think Hamlet to these walls doth come
To tell us what thou hast already guessed?

HORATIO
Readest Will Shakespeare's *Julius Caesar*
And thou would'st know the presence of a ghost
Is ne'er a harbinger of aught but doom.[15]

Enter ghost

HORATIO
But soft, behold! Lo, where it comes again!
I'll see if I can have another word.

Ghost spreads its arms

HORATIO
I beg thee speak; tell me our country's fate.[16]

The cock crows[17]

HORATIO
Speak, phantasm, do not run away!

Exit ghost

18 *The first mention of 'young' Hamlet. Slightly confusing – but Shakespeare intends to pique the audience's curiosity. Is he the new king, we wonder? We shall not wait long to find out he isn't. And is very sore on the subject.*

MARCELLUS

You did it wrong by being so abrupt,
A little more polite you should have been.

HORATIO

Ere the cock crew it was about to speak,
But then it fled so best to 'scape the dawn.
But look, the morn in russet mantle clad
Walks o'er the dew of yon eastward hill.
Methinks 'tis best to go and warn Hamlet
That his dead dad is still in Elsinore.[18]

Exeunt

19 *Cornelius never speaks in the play, even though, as an
    ambassador, he has a significant role in Denmark's affairs.
    He's just there to swell the scene. Whoever played him would
    have juggled multiple other minor roles in the play. The Globe
    had a tight little troupe.*

20 *This is the speech of a brilliant politician. He makes it seem
    as if his marriage to Gertrude was merely political. A union of
    crowns. If so, listeners will assume the relationship is sexually
    blank (no 'enseamed sheets', as Hamlet later disgustedly calls
    them). In fact, the marriage is clearly incestuous. Marrying a
    sister-in-law remained within the degrees of incest until the
    twentieth century. It could, of course, be done for reasons of
    state. But even that was tricky. Henry VIII had to get special
    papal dispensation to marry Catherine of Aragon (his brother
    Arthur's widow). That event led to the Reformation, and
    changed Europe for ever.*

ACT 1, SCENE 2

The great hall of Elsinore castle

Enter Claudius, Gertrude, Hamlet, Polonius, Laertes, Ophelia, Cornelius,[19] Voltemand

CLAUDIUS

    Though we do grieve for this our brother's death
    And feel quite sorry for young Hamlet's loss,
    It can't be good to drown in self-pity;[20]
    Thus we have cheered ourselves by getting wed
    To Gertrude, whom I once 'dear sis' did call.
    So I am king and she can still be queen,
    A nigh-on-perfect nuclear family
    That is content to use the royal 'we'.
    All that is left to do is calm Norway
    And then we can enjoy our reign in peace.
    You, good Cornelius, and you, Voltemand,
    Hie thee away to chat to Fortinbras
    And try to keep him off our Danish ass.

Exeunt Cornelius and Voltemand

21 Laertes, we are informed, did not come back for the funeral
    or the marriage. But his father must have insisted he return
    for the coronation. Laertes is the third only son to feature
    centrally in this most filial of Shakespeare's tragedies.

22 Claudius graciously, and very publicly, yields authority to
    his right-hand man. Doubtless Polonius simpers at the
    compliment. The joke, of course, is on him. Claudius uses the
    old blatherer because he's easily manipulated.

23 Laertes is, we later learn, a student in Paris. Rather more
    exciting than Lutheran Wittenberg. Polonius, well aware
    of Parisian naughtiness, sets a spy to follow Laertes, foxy
    Reynaldo. This is a play worm-holed with espionage.

24 Claudius's term 'son' proclaims publicly that Hamlet will
    be next in line. But why is Young Hamlet not king now?
    Monarchic succession was a topic of obsessive interest to
    Shakespeare and his contemporaries, who were living through
    the anxieties of the Virgin Queen's late years at the turn of
    the century. In Denmark, unlike England, kingship was elective
    – although eldest sons usually succeeded. But not unless they
    were around to do so. And Hamlet wasn't.

25 The pun 'kind' means both 'family member' and 'well
    disposed'. There are a lot of puns in Hamlet – no word should
    be taken at face value.

CLAUDIUS

    And now, Laertes, what's the news with you?
    We hear thou hast a question of the king.

LAERTES

    Now that your coronation is all done,
    I beg your leave to make return to France. [21]

CLAUDIUS

    What says your dad? What says Polonius? [22]

POLONIUS

    Though normally a windbag, I'll be brief:
    I have given Laertes my consent. [23]

CLAUDIUS

    Go, Laertes, make speed to the Rive Gauche.
    But now my cousin Hamlet, and my son— [24]

HAMLET (*aside*)

    A little more than kin, and less than kind. [25]

CLAUDIUS

    Do try to smile; things are not all that bad.

GERTRUDE

    Indeed, my son, make not to be so sad.
    Thou surely knows that every life must end,
    And thy dear father had a good innings.

26 *The court is in high fashion, in honour of their king's wedding. Hamlet is still, months on, in funereal black. Protocol would only require him to be in 'half mourning' at this stage – if that. Gertrude, of course, will be in wedding gear.*

27 *The ban on Wittenberg is not, of course, because Claudius wants his darling 'son', as he's just described him, close to home and family. He wants to keep an eye on the young pretender, lest Hamlet hatches a plot to displace him – as Laertes later will. Elsinore has the Jacobean equivalent of CCTV all over the place. In the palace, Prince Hamlet will be 'safe', neutered. Killable, if necessary.*

28 *His acquiescence is odd. His love for Ophelia, whom we have yet to meet, is a possible reason for staying. But why, a passionate student, would he give up university to moon about Elsinore's corridors?*

29 *Back to the paternal 'thee' and 'thou', rather than the more formal 'you' used earlier. He's now dad, not King Claudius. The villain uses these tricks of the trade cleverly.*

30 *Richard Burbage, who starred as Hamlet, was famously plump. Some editors, with that in mind, prefer 'sullied' – 'dirty'. The word 'thaw' again stresses this is icy winter.*

HAMLET

I do not dress in black just to impress
How much I miss my dad now he is dead.
My grief's more deep than any passing shroud,
'Tis more like a life-threatening malaise.[26]

CLAUDIUS

Come on, old boy, do try and get a grip.
Your grief has time and place and this ain't it.
When all is said and done, your dad's no more.
These things do happen; just get over it.
To give you cheer, I'll tell you what we'll do.
I'll make you our successor to the throne;
Fairer than that, I really cannot say.
Just one condition I do make of thee:
Thou don't return to school in Germany.[27]

HAMLET

I shall obey and not to uni go.[28]

CLAUDIUS

Thou art most kind, I thank thee for thy pledge.
Now try to have some fun; be not a drudge.[29]

Exeunt all but Hamlet

HAMLET

O that this too too solid flesh would melt[30]
Thaw and resolve itself into a dew.
Or that the Everlasting had not fixed

31 In point of fact, there is no mandate in the Bible against self-slaughter. And as his Roman plays indicate, Shakespeare himself admired the act, as performed by the ancients. Brutus's suicide is the fittingly noble termination to a noble life, Marc Antony tells us. Nonetheless, Catholic doctrine, from Aquinas onwards, anathematised suicide, and canon law prohibited the act as a mortal sin. The term 'canon' here (i.e. Church law) was very much RC lingo. Did Shakespeare have Catholic sympathies? Critics are divided on the subject.

32 Timeline is important here, but not entirely easy to follow. Old Hamlet died suddenly. Stung, improbably, by a serpent. The news would have taken time to get to Wittenberg (hundreds of miles from Elsinore), and Hamlet would have taken time to gallop back to Elsinore. Before Hamlet could get back, Claudius had been elected king. After the election came the coronation and the wedding. All suspiciously fast. Our best guess is that it's four months since the murder, although Hamlet says it is less than two months since the funeral. Shakespeare's plays are elastic about such details and they rarely trouble audiences as much as they do editors and critics.

33 Women have a thin time of it in this most hairy-chested play. There are only two female speaking parts. This first soliloquy (is Hamlet talking or thinking?) has characterised Hamlet as 'melancholic' and a 'malcontent' – two stereotypes on the Jacobean stage.

34 Has Horatio just arrived? We learn that he was around for the funeral and the wedding, yet Hamlet has not seen him till now. Odd.

35 He does not, even having witnessed the apparition himself, go all the way with the ghost thesis. Yet.

His canon 'gainst self-slaughter.[31] O God! God!
How weary, stale, flat and unprofitable
Seem to me all the uses of this world!
'Tis but two months since my dear dad hath passed,
And yet my mum to Claudius is wed
And romps quite freely in the lech's bed.[32]
Let me not think on't; frailty, thy name is woman![33]
Yet I must hold my tongue, not say a word.

Enter Horatio, Marcellus and Barnardo

HAMLET

'Tis good to see thee back from Wittenberg;
But what is your affair in Elsinore?

HORATIO

A bit of this and that and nothing more.[34]

HAMLET

Methinks you came to see my mother wed.

HORATIO

Well, it did merge into the funeral
Of thy dear father, whom I lovest well.
Talking of which, these men did see a ghost
They swore was a dead ringer for your pa.
And when last night I joined them on their watch,
I must admit the same thought I did have.[35]

36 Why sorrowful? Because of Gertrude marrying so soon, we assume, before his body was decently cold.

37 If he were wearing armour and a helmet, only his eyes would be visible through the visor.
     The use of ghosts in drama goes back to Seneca, and had become somewhat hackneyed on the Jacobean stage. There were various schools of thought about them generally. Protestantism, England's and Denmark's state religion, gave ghosts little credence. Folklore (plenty of that around Stratford-upon-Avon) believed in them with pagan credulity. Most interesting here, however, is the Catholic notion of purgatory, or limbo, in which a ghost could be held in a kind of waiting room between earth and heaven or hell, burning (being 'purged') in daylight hours, wandering at night. That purgatorial waiting room, we assume, is where Old Hamlet is currently kicking his ghostly heels. Later he will confirm the fact.

38 At this stage, Hamlet only suspects 'foul play'. Not murder. The sport he would be thinking about is fencing (stabbing an opponent in the back, for example, or using an unbuttoned weapon). He's an accomplished fencer, we shall later learn. And it's foul play in a fencing match that kills him.

HAMLET

What, looked he frowningly?

HORATIO

A countenance more in sorrow than in anger.[36]

HAMLET

Pray tell me more. What look was in his eye?
What did he tell thee of his ghostly state?[37]

HORATIO

Though I implored him, he refused to speak
And beetled off the moment the cock crowed.
I beg you, this night, join us on our guard.
Perhaps he will to his son offer words.

HAMLET

That will I do, I'll see you three anon.

Exeunt all but Hamlet

HAMLET

If father armed be, all cannot be well.
Foul play there hath been in this Danish hell.[38]

Exit

39 The relationship between Hamlet and Ophelia is already being gossiped about in Elsinore, we gather. Laertes makes the point that men of Prince Hamlet's status may not, as 'unvalued' people do, marry for love. Although they can philander quite serenely.

40 The later mad scenes and Ophelia's raunchy ditties suggest that the damage has already been done and they have 'gone all the way', although critics have been unable to make up their minds whether she is a virgin or a 'maid no more'.

ACT 1, SCENE 3

Elsinore, a private room

Enter Laertes and his sister Ophelia

LAERTES

My bags are packed, I come to say farewell,
Though first I must give thee some good advice
About young Hamlet: he is not your type.[39]

OPHELIA

Be not my aunt of agony. Be gone!

LAERTES

Forgive me, sis, I have to speak my mind.
I do believe that Hamlet is a cad
Who wants you for your body, not your mind.
Being of royal blood, he'll not you wed
Though if you let him, he'll take you to bed.
Remember, then, always to constant be
And let him not sweet-talk you to undress.[40]

41 *Not so fast, a paternal sermon is coming. Polonius never wastes a captive audience.*

42 *He tells his son to be off, then keeps the restless young man waiting interminably. Pure Polonius. What is ironic is that his 'To thine own self be true' has become a universal moral precept. It's contaminated, of course, by coming from the mouth of a total hypocrite.*

OPHELIA

Why, thanks for nothing, bruv. I'm not a slut
And I do think that Hamlet loves me well.
Methinks the pot doth call the kettle black,
For thou wilt get thy end away abroad.

LAERTES

Is that the time? I really must be off.[41]

Enter Polonius

POLONIUS

Yet here, Laertes? Aboard, aboard, for shame!
Keep these few precepts in thy memory.
Be thou familiar, but by no means vulgar.
Do not a quarrel make, yet if thou finds
A bloke bears arms at thee, do not back down.
Neither a borrower nor a lender be;
For loan oft loses both itself and friend,
And borrowing dulls the edge of husbandry.
This above all: to thine own self be true,
And it must follow, as the night the day,
Thou canst not then be false to anyone.[42]

LAERTES

Dear father, you don't half go on and on,
Yet I would not deny thy poetry.
And with that thought, I bid you both adieu.

Exit Laertes

43 As mentioned in note 14, Shakespeare had no surviving son (a matter of grief, one can assume), but he had daughters (a matter of occasional irritation, one can assume). Hamneth's twin sister, Judith, would have been fifteen in 1600 – Ophelia's age. There may be some self-mockery here in Polonius's totally inefficacious advice. Young women do not listen to their fathers.

POLONIUS

Tell me, sweet daughter, what your bruv did say?[43]

OPHELIA

I'm sure that it will come as no surprise;
He begged me no more see my prince Hamlet.

POLONIUS

I do concur with mine own son's advice,
For Hamlet is a bad lad, no mistake.
The prince doth want one thing, one thing alone;
He doth not care about thy innocence.
Though he may tell thee that he doth love thee,
'Tis in thy pants he really wants to be.
Thou wilt not ever be a royal bride.
I do beseech thee, keep him at arm's length.

Exeunt

44 Ghosts, being bloodless, are traditionally associated with cold spots. They are also supposed to be able to drop the mercury to goose-pimple temperature when they are around.

45 'We'll teach you to drink deep, ere you depart,' Hamlet tells Horatio. But Horatio doesn't depart from Elsinore. On the battlements the two men wait impatiently – it 'lacks of twelve'. The ghost, however, will be punctual.

ACT 1, SCENE 4

The gun platform

Enter Hamlet, Horatio and Marcellus

HORATIO
We'll catch our death here high up on this keep.

HAMLET
Ay, that we will, 'tis freezing cold for sure.
Yet 't'will be worth it if the ghost doth come.[44]

HORATIO
What noise is that which comes from down below?

HAMLET
Why 'tis my uncle and his loyal men;
Each night they getteth pissed, till they can't stand.
It is an affliction well known to Danes,
Give them a drink and they'll get out of hand.[45]

Enter ghost

46 He sees his father, even beyond death, as the real
    king of Denmark.

47 Marcellus and Horatio attempt to restrain Hamlet physically.
    It prompts his violent remark, 'By heaven, I'll make a ghost of
    him who lets [i.e. prevents] me!' His sword is drawn.

48 The belief was that all ghosts were either demonic or diabolic.
    The humans are on the high-point bastion of the castle
    with a sheer drop into the sea below. There is a theory that
    Shakespeare, in his 'lost years', may have gone to sea. If so, he
    might have seen towering Elsinore (Kronborg castle).

HORATIO
   See there, my lord, this way the ghost doth come.

HAMLET
   Angels and ministers of grace defend us!
   Thou hast told the truth, I know that now,
   It is the very image of my dad.[46]
   What can it mean? His corpse hath left the grave
   To cast a spectral presence 'fore our eyes?
   I would, I will have words and speak with him.

Ghost beckons Hamlet

HORATIO
   It beckons you to go away with it.

MARCELLUS
   Stay here, my lord, it is a threatening ghost.
   If it nearer comes, I'll run it through.

HAMLET
   It will not speak unless I follow it.

HORATIO
   Do not go, I beg thee, noble lord.[47]
   What if it is not friendly after all,
   And merely seeks to throw you from the cliff?[48]

HAMLET
> Why should I fear my own mortality
> When mine own soul for e'er immortal be?
> I beg you do not stop me. Unhand me!
> Now with my father's spirit I will go.

MARCELLUS
> Something is rotten in the state of Denmark.

Exeunt Hamlet and ghost

HORATIO
> On your head be it. I'll keep watch from here.

Exeunt

49 I.e. pay attention to what I say. A father's comment, one notes.

50 This is one of the more tantalising speeches in the play. The
    'flames of purgatory' comment indicates that Hamlet's world
    exists within a larger Catholic cosmos, and critics have read
    a lot into it about Shakespeare's covert religious sympathies.
    Anne of Denmark was suspected of Catholic conversion.
    Catholics were, of course, persecuted under James's monarchy,
    as they had been under Elizabeth's. But why, one might
    wonder, is Old Hamlet in purgatory, having his sins purged
    away by flames? The (not entirely convincing) reason he gives
    is that he was 'untimely' killed, 'not shriving time allowed' and
    'full of bread'. Technicalities. He also briefly mentions certain
    unspecified 'vile crimes'. Every king has a few.

51 What, pray, is 'natural' murder? 'Unnatural' murder could
    refer to Claudius committing the unforgivable crime of Cain,
    fratricide (something that worries Claudius later, as his
    chickens come home to roost). Or murder to pursue incest.

ACT 1, SCENE 5

The walls of Elsinore castle

Enter ghost and Hamlet

HAMLET
Where wilt thou lead me? Speak. I'll go no further.

GHOST
Mark me.[49]

HAMLET
       I will.

GHOST
           My time is almost come,
When I to flames of purgatory must go.
For ere I died, I never had the chance
To confess my sins and receive God's grace.[50]
But 'fore I go, there's news that thou should'st know,
So that thou can revenge what thou dost hear,
Since I was murdered most unnaturally.[51]

52 *This one word is the trigger for what follows, hinging on another word: 'revenge'. The revenge play was a popular dramatic genre on the Jacobean stage – always located in foreign (less civilised) countries. There is, in the standard plot, no legal authority the aggrieved revenger can call on for 'justice'. Merely the law of retaliation. It puts Hamlet in an exquisite dilemma. He is being asked to do something the Almighty prohibits. He'll go straight to hell, without passing purgatory, for eternity. Elizabethan and Jacobean civil law also saw murderous revenge as a threat to the very existence of the state. It was punished as murder. Hamlet is no thoughtless thug. What should he do? Interestingly, Denmark is recorded as being more tolerant of the law of retaliation than other European countries (the Viking spirit?).*

53 *Of course, the cover story is that he was stung by a serpent. Poisonous snakes are few and far between in Denmark, even at the height of summer. Claudius could surely have come up with something more convincing.*

54 *Those interested in poisoning point out that poison dropped down the ear will do nothing more than clear up any residual wax.*

55 *It has the force of a bombshell when the ghost accuses Claudius of being not merely 'incestuous' (i.e. marrying a deceased sibling's spouse) but 'adulterate'. What this means is that there was something illicit going on before Old Hamlet died, in direct contravention of the divine seventh commandment. Whether or not there was actual adultery is, however, never made entirely clear. And why 'adulterate' (which can merely mean 'spoiled'), not 'adulterous'?*

HAMLET
Murder?[52]

GHOST
Murder most foul, and done by Uncle Claud.
Having a kip I was in the orchard—[53]

HAMLET
How come thou chose to have a sleep outdoors
When Elsinore is wreathed in frost and ice?

GHOST
'Tis not the time to pick holes in the plot,
I beg you concentrate on my story.
For as I slept your uncle did appear
And tipped the strongest poison in my ear.[54]
To make things worse, my wife he then did wed.
I cannot bear the thought of my Gertrude
Wrapped in the arms of that poisonous snake.
I beg thee, Hamlet, as my torment grows
Let not the royal bed of Denmark be
A couch for luxury and damned incest.
Claud is naught but an adulterate beast,[55]
Take thy revenge, howe'er thou thinkest fit.
Just one last favour of thee I do beg:
Thou dost not harm a hair of Gertie's head.
Adieu, adieu! Hamlet, remember me.

Exit ghost

56 *Ever the geeky student, our Hamlet. He has a notebook (or wax tablet) and pencil (or, possibly, slate and chalk) by him at all times. But why he should need to make notes now is not entirely clear. Having a long conversation with your dead father would seem to be fairly memorable. But Shakespeare is making an important point – Hamlet does not act, he merely thinks about acting. We can imagine him scribbling down: 'Vengeance? Must look up what Aquinas says.'*

57 *'Honest' means two things: 'real ghost' and 'truth-telling ghost' (i.e. not demonic/diabolic).*

58 *What this indicates, theatrically, is that the ghost left smartly (now you see him, now you don't) by a trapdoor, landing on a mattress. He is now under the boards.*

HAMLET

    I do promise I will remember this,
    I will not rest until thy will be done.
    And just in case my memory doth slip
    I'll make a note of it in my handbook.[56]

Enter Horatio and Marcellus

HORATIO

    Ah there you are! Thank God thou art alive.
    Pray tell me what the hell is going on.

HAMLET

    My lips are sealed, I cannot say a word.
    Just this I'll say: it was an honest ghost[57]
    Whom I did meet upon these battlements.
    Now swear one thing upon the pain of death:
    Never make known what you have seen tonight.

GHOST (*from under stage*)[58]

    Swear.

HORATIO

    Propose the oath, I'll swear it happily.

HAMLET

    Swear by my sword you'll mention none of this.

GHOST

    Swear.

59 *Hamlet does not have a Bible with him. But the hilt of his sword is, for the purpose, a cross. Why, one wonders, is the ghost so keen on the three of them swearing? And why can Marcellus and Horatio not hear what the ghost is shouting? Clearly, since the ghost has been seen by all three of them, it is 'real'. But – and this is a suspicion which is stoked up during the course of the play – is Hamlet losing his wits, hearing things and talking to himself? The first signs of madness.*

HORATIO

  O day and night, but this is wondrous strange!

HAMLET

  And therefore as a stranger give it welcome.
  There are more things in heaven and earth, Horatio,
  Than are dreamt of in your philosophy.

HORATIO

  'Tis not my fault I studied PPE;
  It's not that big a deal, happ'ly I'll swear.

HAMLET

  Now that you hold my sword, I'll also ask
  That should I start to look and act most strange
  You will behave as if I were normal.[59]

GHOST

  Swear.

HORATIO

  I am content to swear these things to you.

HAMLET

  Then we are done here and must go indoors,
  For, like the blessed ghost, we're out of time.

Exeunt

60 *At last we see the real Polonius – to his own self being true. Reynaldo ('the foxy one') is sent ostensibly to give Laertes letters and money; in fact, he is being sent to spy on him.*

ACT 2, SCENE 1

A state room in the castle

Enter Polonius and Reynaldo

POLONIUS
Go forth to Paris, there to watch my son.
I fear he's prone to getting pissed in bars.[60]

REYNALDO
I will, my lord.

POLONIUS
Dim inter-railing students on the lash
Get into trouble and lose all their cash.

REYNALDO
I get it, my lord.

POLONIUS
Make sure he stays away from the red lights
And easy women riddled with VD.
If thou dost fear he loseth all resolve,
Then get in first and take one for the team.

61 In early printed stage directions to this scene, he is described
     as 'Old Polonius'. Later, Hamlet will make some cruel jokes
     about Polonius's age. He displays the twin stage stereotypes
     of a man of advanced years, at times a wise old man, at other
     times an old fool. He forgets what he is saying here. Incipient
     cognitive impairment?

62 Polonius also encourages Reynaldo to tell lies about his
     son, to elicit salacious gossip. We are learning about the
     unscrupulous lengths Polonius (and Claudius) will go to in
     statecraft. And personal relations.

63 Never to be seen or heard of again.

REYNALDO

    I said, I get it, my lord.

POLONIUS

    Mmm. Now where was I? I was sure I was going to
    ask you to do something else . . .[61]

REYNALDO

    I think you've just about covered it, my lord.

POLONIUS

    Stay close to him, but ne'er so close he thinks
    That thou art paid to keep him company.[62]

REYNALDO

    Have you finished, my lord?

POLONIUS

    I think I must have, now you mention it,
    All that's left to do is fare thee well.

REYNALDO

    Farewell then, my lord.

        Exit Reynaldo[63]
        Enter Ophelia

OPHELIA

    My lord, as I was sewing in my closet,
    Prince Hamlet burst in looking most distressed,

64 The fact that he can come into her private quarters in a state of undress suggests this is not the first time he has been alone with her there. (That lovers in extremis may be recognised by their untrussed garters is also referred to by Shakespeare in Love's Labour's Lost.) But is Hamlet putting on an act? He was wearing smart funeral clothes a short time ago. Interestingly, Ophelia has no female attendants or companions. And, of course, no mother to protect her.

65 Is Hamlet mad? He may be merely pretending to have lost his mind, to give himself time to think about (1) how to test the truth of what the ghost has said, and (2) how to set up an appropriate strategy for revenge. In plays of this kind, the revenge must be ingenious and artful ('mousetrap' clever). Sometimes (viz. serpents in orchards and poison down the lughole) it can be too clever.

66 The cameo can be read three ways. As a perpetrator of revenge and future regicide, Hamlet can no longer be a lover (assuming he lives, which is highly unlikely). But he cannot confide in Ophelia, the daughter of Polonius (who, as this scene shows, tells her father all), why their affair must end, whatever the consequences for her (is she, perhaps, pregnant?). On the other hand, he could be having the same kind of lover's collywobbles that afflict Romeo in the opening scenes of that tragedy. But why have we seen no sign of this in his previous soliloquies and asides? Or, most likely, Hamlet is throwing up a deliberate smokescreen to deceive Polonius and Claudius and give himself time and space to think things through. ('The poor fellow's love-mad. He's not planning to cut the king's throat. Oh no.')

67 We have no doubt, since Ophelia does everything her father tells her, that she has followed his earlier instructions and dumped Hamlet. Feminist critics have made informative explorations into the character of Ophelia – a woman who turns mistreatment by every man in her life into self-harm.

His shirt undone, his tights tatty and torn,
His eyes were vacant, his brow all sweaty,
One might believe that he had seen a ghost.[64]

POLONIUS

I fear the prince is mad with love for you.[65]

OPHELIA

He held my hand, his head upon my lap,
Then he did sigh and shake most piteously.
And when I asked him what his problem was
He ran away and failed to say a word.[66]

POLONIUS

Hamlet is too far gone, that much is clear,
His love for thee more ardent than I guessed.
Be careful that thy darling buds of May
Do not temptation make for his foreplay.
The king must hear of these strange actions:
Canst thou be sure thou hast not led him on?

OPHELIA

I did as I was told and nothing more;[67]
Not least because his madness drives me mad.

POLONIUS

Then we must go straightway unto the king
To let him know his nephew's lost the plot.

Exeunt

68 Claudius's suspicions are growing apace. Hamlet has not responded to trumpets, kettledrums and cannon, or to public proclamations that he's next in line. It's clear that these two students (Germans, their names indicate) have been invited from Wittenberg not as guests but to serve as spies and informers. Claudius, ever the schemer, has done his research. Horatio, for example (another best friend from Wittenberg), would be unbribable.

69 How corrupt are these two? What do they expect, after they have established themselves as courtiers, from the king of another country? Later on, Hamlet implies they see careers for themselves as international spies. Shakespeare knew one such – the playwright Christopher Marlowe. It beats studying philosophy. And the pay may be good. There are now four Wittenberg undergrads playing truant in Elsinore.

ACT 2, SCENE 2

The great hall of Elsinore castle

Enter Claudius, Gertrude, Rosencrantz and Guildenstern

CLAUDIUS
Welcome, dear Rosencrantz and Guildenstern!
We have a job you both might well enjoy.
Our son Hamlet hath become most moody,
His scowl is fierce, he barely says a word;
Our nephew's not himself, we know not why.[68]

GERTRUDE
You'd almost think his father had just died,
Or that his mum had remarried too soon.
So, as we know, he trusts you both as friends;
We do entreat you gain his confidence
And come and tell us what is going on.

ROSENCRANTZ
Most willingly we follow your desires.

GUILDENSTERN
Indeed we do, your wish is our command.[69]

70 We remind ourselves that Fortinbras, son of the late king of Norway (killed by Old Hamlet), is nephew to the current king of Norway. Symmetries present themselves. Hamlet is nephew to the king of Denmark. The king of Norway (name unknown) is, we are informed, old, frail, and – we deduce – under the influence of his nephew. It is dangerous for Denmark that Claudius is being distracted by the domestic Hamlet problem. His eye should be on international matters.

71 It's easy to forget what a European play Hamlet is. Shakespeare here points to the fluid alliances and hostilities which flared up for two centuries or more between expansionist Norway, Denmark, Sweden and Poland (Russia was also drawn in occasionally). The most recent outright conflicts were the Great Northern and Livonian wars of the 1580s. It's easy to deduce, with a Danish-British queen up the river, why Shakespeare should have allocated precious stage time to such scenes. Claudius, incidentally, is being duped by the Norwegians. His eye is off the ball.

Exeunt Rosencrantz and Guildenstern
Enter Polonius

POLONIUS

Th'ambassadors from Norway are returned.

CLAUDIUS

Well, that was quick, they left but hours ago.
Bid them come in and tell us what they've learnt.

POLONIUS

That will I do, and when they both have left
I'd like a word, because I'm sure I've found
The very cause of Hamlet's lunacy.

Enter Voltemand

VOLTEMAND

Good news I bring to you, my noble lord.
The king of Norway hath got his own way;[70]
After much persuasion, Fortinbras
Hath promised not to go to war with us;
His blood lust will be satisfied with Poles.[71]

CLAUDIUS

That Denmark has been spared is a relief.
Wish Fortinbras good luck against the Poles.

Exit Voltemand

72 Polonius's garrulity, which gets worse as the play progresses, suggests that he is drifting into senile decay a lot faster than he thinks Hamlet is going love-crazy. An alternative theory is that he is embarrassed that he is indirectly responsible for this crisis (not having stepped in earlier). The Polonius family is not rich or titled. And he's well past his sell-by date as a plenipotentiary royal aide.

73 Gertrude is a sensible woman of few words. What's wrong with Hamlet, she is asked by Claudius. 'Our hasty marriage,' she replies. She's at least partly right on that score. She does not know that Claudius killed her husband – or does she suspect? That serpent-in-the-orchard story is fishy. Later we discover she hoped Hamlet would marry Ophelia, which suggests the two women were close.

74 Polonius, spy that he is, has no scruples about raiding his daughter's private correspondence. Hamlet knows that, of course.

75 Critics note, some with surprise, what a feeble missive Hamlet sends Ophelia – presumably evidence of game-playing on his part. Ophelia's speeches suggest she is commendably literate, and worthy of something more eloquent. Hamlet, incidentally, has three letters read out in the course of the play – a Shakespearean record.

POLONIUS

    Now will I tell thee why thy son is weird,
    Why day is day, night night, and time is time,
    Were nothing but to waste night, day and time,
    Therefore, since brevity is the soul of wit,
    And tediousness the limbs and outward flourishes,
    I will be brief: your noble son is mad.[72]

GERTRUDE

    Make haste, old man, and get thee to the point.[73]

POLONIUS

    Why, Madam, I do not circumlocute,
    For when I say he's mad, he is just that.
    His madness is a defect of the heart,
    Since in his wooing of Ophelia
    He hath been sending senseless billets doux.[74]

Reads the letter

'O celestial Ophelia, I think you're gorgeous and I
really, really love you. I'm sorry I'm not very good at
chatting you up but I'm a bit messed up and no one
really understands me. Yours, Hamlet.'[75]

GERTRUDE

    How did your daughter make reply to this?

76 How long has passed since the prohibition, when Laertes
(Ophelia's protector) left for France? If Polonius's explanation
is to hold any water, weeks must have passed. But they can't
have done: Hamlet's only very recently back from Wittenberg.
Critics have suggested that in reading, or watching,
Shakespeare's plays we should utilise, where necessary, a
'double time-scheme'. It's necessary here, for plausibility.

77 Polonius is by now sinking even lower in the audience's
estimation. Here he is proposing to pimp out his daughter
(unwillingly, but dutifully, on her part). The word 'loose' is
damning. The 'arras' (a wall-hanging to keep out draughts,
often lavishly embroidered) plays such an important role in
Hamlet that it should have an entry in the dramatis personae.

78 Claudius is sceptical. His main motive is to eliminate this
fanciful speculation of Polonius.

79 No character in Shakespeare, with the possible exception
of Prospero in The Tempest, has their nose in a book more
persistently than Hamlet. Prospero's books contain magic,
Hamlet's philosophy. Hamlet's book here, of course, may be
intended to disguise the murderous act he has in mind.

POLONIUS

When I did tell her he was not her type
She did politely reject his advance.
And once Hamlet did know he'd been turned down
He lost all touch with reason and went mad.[76]

CLAUDIUS

Art thou certain of thine observations?

POLONIUS

Indeed I am, and content to prove it.
Sometimes he walks for hours on his own;
At such a time I'll loose my daughter to him,
Be you and I behind an arras then.[77]

CLAUDIUS

That sounds a plan. Let's give it our best shot.[78]

Exeunt Claudius and Gertrude
Enter Hamlet, reading a book[79]

POLONIUS

How does my good lord Hamlet?

HAMLET

Ah! It's the fish-monger.

POLONIUS

I think you've got the wrong man.

80 *Hamlet's rudeness is somewhat out of character. Or, at least, one would like to think it is. He is either furious that Polonius has barred access to Ophelia, or (as some productions assume) he has caught a glimpse of Claudius behind the arras.*

81 *Hamlet riddles. He knows precisely what Polonius is up to. But he keeps in the air the possibility that he is, if not mad, distracted, and incapable of giving a straight answer to a straight question.*

82 *He is reading satire. A satire on old men. Or so he claims. Most probably Machiavelli's* The Prince. *Prince Hamlet is getting very cunning.*

83 *Polonius affects to be concerned about Hamlet, and wants to get him out of the cold air. Most likely, of course, he wants to get him away to set up Ophelia and the arras affair.*

HAMLET

There's nothing wrong with being a pimp. Do you
have a daughter?[80]

POLONIUS (*aside*)

I'm not sure what he's on about. He said he didn't
know me, yet he then remembered I have a daughter.
He's totally lost it.
– What are you reading?

HAMLET

Words, words, words.[81]

POLONIUS

I meant, what book are you reading?

HAMLET

The Prince. It's named after me. You won't have heard
of it. It's about how useless and stupid old men are.
You'd be as old as I am if you were younger.[82]

POLONIUS (*aside*)

Though this be madness, yet there is method in't.
– Will you come out of the air?[83]

HAMLET

Only to the grave.

84 The aside is directed to the audience.

85 Leave/life. A pun. We are not sure how differently words were
   pronounced in Shakespeare's day. Quite possibly 'leave' was
   pronounced with an 'f' sound, making it more like 'life'.

86 The undergraduate banter descends rapidly into the bawdy
   of the ale-house. Rosencrantz and Guildenstern are testing
   the mad-for-love theory by going straight to sex. They are,
   of course, respectful (in this place, perhaps not back in
   Wittenberg) of Hamlet's superior rank. Lots of 'my lord'
   and deference.

POLONIUS

Well that is out of the air of a kind, I suppose.
(*aside*) Poor boy! He's really not at all well. I'll
disappear to engineer a meeting between him and
my daughter.[84]

– I take my leave.

HAMLET

You can take my life if you want.[85] Farewell, you
old bore.

Exit Polonius
Enter Rosencrantz and Guildenstern

HAMLET

What brings you here?

ROSENCRANTZ

We were hoping to pick up some girls.

GUILDENSTERN

But so far they are keeping their privates private.[86]

HAMLET

Isn't that always the way? But you must be really
desperate to come here. Denmark's a prison.

ROSENCRANTZ

I wouldn't say that.

87 *Hamlet is not being unguarded. He is testing them. They fail the test.*

88 *Testing them again. They can't leave. They have a mission.*

HAMLET

Whatever. For there is nothing either good or bad,
but thinking makes it so. To me it is a prison. I hate
this place.[87]

GUILDENSTERN

You're a bit limited in your ambition. Try and
cheer up.

HAMLET

I can't. I'm lousy company. Find someone better to
hang out with.[88]

ROSENCRANTZ

We came to be with you.

HAMLET

Pull the other one. No one would want to see me in
this state. Someone told you to come here, didn't they?

GUILDENSTERN

Why would they do that?

HAMLET

Don't treat me like an idiot.

ROSENCRANTZ

OK, OK. We were sent for.

89 This may give us a clue to the book Hamlet is reading so
    ostentatiously. It's plausibly suggested that this speech
    is a gloss on Montaigne's similar high-flown rhapsodies
    in his essays. The most influential critic of present times,
    Stephen Greenblatt, has made much of Shakespeare's debt to
    Montaigne, contradicting T. S. Eliot's contention that Hamlet
    is no philosopher, beyond a few commonplaces.

90 It was routine for London companies to go on tour to make
    money, or when the theatres were closed by plague. It was not
    something enjoyed by the actors. This scene reminds us that
    Elsinore is in the sticks.

91 It's later evident that Hamlet does know the troupe and their
    repertoire. It defies logic, of course, that they've come from
    either Wittenberg or Copenhagen. We're temporarily on a
    different planet: Southwark, 1599.

HAMLET

I knew it. The king and queen have had enough of
my moods. Well, tough. I'm pissed off and that's that.
I can't stand this place and I can't stand the people
round here. God! What piece of work is a man! And
a woman, for that matter. What is this quintessence of
dust? I'd rather just be on my own.[89]

ROSENCRANTZ

Then you're going to be in for a pretty miserable time.
On the way here, we bumped into a troupe of actors
who were hoping to entertain you.[90]

HAMLET

Are they any good?

ROSENCRANTZ

I doubt it. They've only come because a bunch of
kids are a big hit in their own town. But they're all
we've got.[91]

HAMLET

Things go out of fashion fast round here.

GUILDENSTERN

Anyway, there they are.

92 Critics have tied themselves in knots trying to work out
the hawk/handsaw business. One of the more ingenious
interpretations is that handsaw = heronshaw, i.e. a bird which
isn't a hawk. A scribal or printer's error. This suggests that
Hamlet has rumbled that R&G are 'hawks', spying on him.
He is playing with them, knowing that whatever he says will
get back to Claudius: he wants him to know that the game of
vengeance is now afoot.

93 An in-joke. Shakespeare, like other dramatists of the period,
liked mixing genres – as in tragi-comedy (e.g. Measure
for Measure). One of his favourite collaborators, Thomas
Middleton, was a master of the generic cocktail.

HAMLET
    Thanks. I'm sorry I wasn't more welcoming. But you
    should know that my mother has misled you. I am
    but mad north-north-west. When the wind is southerly,
    I know a hawk from a handsaw.[92]

Enter Polonius

POLONIUS
    Exciting news, my lord.

HAMLET
    The old half-wit's come to tell me the players
    have arrived.

POLONIUS
    I come to tell thee that the finest actors in Denmark
    have come to entertain thee. Drama, history, rom-com,
    sci-fi – you name it, they can do it.[93]

HAMLET
    Maybe a play about a daughter
    Who learnt a lesson that I taught her.

POLONIUS
    Do stop going on about daughters. You're
    unnerving me.

Enter the players

94 *The boy-actor whom he saw on the stage a short while ago (playing women's parts) is now 'valanced' – he has a beard. And, of course, his voice will have broken. His womanising is over. Queer-studies criticism has alerted readers and audiences to the homosexual currents inherent in the womanless Elizabethan-Jacobean acting profession.*

95 *Priam is significant. He is, as fathers go, the most heroically fatherly figure in classical literature, with one hundred sons (daughters don't count) – twenty of them from the 'teeming loins' of Hecuba. And he is killed in the destruction of Troy by Achilles' son, Pyrrhus, in an act of revenge for killing his father (sound familiar?). Why has Hamlet selected this play? Because Polonius is watching and will report back to Claudius. ('Revenge is on your nephew's mind, my liege, it's even evident in the plays he's thinking of.')*

96 *Hamlet's delay in killing Claudius can be explained in various ways. He may still be in two minds as to whether he should believe the ghost: the 'mousetrap' supports that view. He may be giving thought to a fiendishly ingenious stratagem – he makes a few comments on that necessity. And, of course, there is the psychoanalytic, Freudian theory. See note 132 for more on this.*

HAMLET

You are welcome, masters; welcome, all. Oh God! It's
you. You've aged a bit since I last saw you. And you
too, my lady. No longer the spring chicken. Anyway,
give us a speech.[94]

PLAYER 1

Anything in particular?

HAMLET

I seem to remember you doing something about
Dido and Aeneas in which King Priam gets whacked
after a horse gets into Troy. How did it go?[95]
'The rugged Pyrrhus, he whose sable arms . . .'
Ring any bells?

PLAYER 1

Thus into Ilium the horse did go,
And out did jump big Pyrrhus and his sword,
Straight into Priam's house he then did rush,
To slit his throat and stab him in the heart.

POLONIUS

This is a bit long and gory.

HAMLET

I'm loving it. Carry on.[96]

97 *The player is so into his part, method style, that he is genuinely emotional. Hamlet, who is torn between acting (playing a part) and acting (doing something), is fascinated.*

98 *And tell Claudius what is coming his way. What happened to Priam.*

99 *An Italian play. Despite heroic efforts by critics, no work of that name has ever been identified.*

PLAYER 1

Then Hecuba did spy her hubby's blood
Upon her most precious Turkish carpet.
And she did howl and wail throughout the night,
For cleaner was there none beneath the sink.

POLONIUS

Give him a break. He's tearing up.[97]

HAMLET

That is enough, good sir. You run along now,
Polonius, and make sure the actors have some food.[98]

Exit Polonius

HAMLET (*aside*)

Thank goodness Polonius is too dim to notice that I
had forgotten to be mad just then.
– You, sir! Do you know *The Murder of Gonzago*?[99]

PLAYER 1

Ay!

HAMLET

Great. I've just got a few lines I'd like you to add.

Exeunt players

100 Elizabethans (following ancient Greek theory) believed the liver generated blood for the body. A pale liver correlated with cowardice and feebleness.

101 Hamlet goes to these elaborate lengths (the play within the play) to prove to himself that Claudius is guilty. Or, since Claudius is clearly brazen enough to keep the murder to himself, to let the murderer know that Hamlet is on to him.

HAMLET

Note how the actor wept for Hecuba
When she to him was nothing but a role.
So what a lily-livered wimp am I,
That doth do nothing when I have just cause;[100]
If I were man enough, I'd take revenge.
Though p'raps 'tis best to give myself a break,
For I still lack sufficient evidence.
Here's what I'll do: I'll weave into the play
The murder that my father's ghost did tell.
And if my dear mama and Uncle Claud
Are shocked by what they see upon the stage,
Then will their guilt be visible to all,
And I've just cause for making merry hell.[101]

Exit

102   *The word 'act', with its two senses – 'to do something' and 'to pretend to do, or be, something' – is crucial to the action of* Hamlet. *Claudius, until this point in the play, has been inscrutable. In the second half, we shall get more and more inside his mind, seeing his motives, his guilt, his ambitions.*

103   *R&G are not, we can deduce, that bright. Otherwise they would warn Claudius that there is something very dangerous going on in Hamlet's brain. In his early play* Rosencrantz and Guildenstern are Dead, *Tom Stoppard has great fun with their complex stupidities and their mortifying awareness that they are stupid. Or superfluous. Or the human equivalent of wall-hangings.*

ACT 3, SCENE 1

The great hall of Elsinore castle

Enter Claudius, Gertrude, Polonius, Ophelia,
Rosencrantz and Guildenstern

CLAUDIUS
Did Hamlet tell you why he acts so mad?[102]

ROSENCRANTZ
He doth admit he feeleth not himself.

GUILDENSTERN
Yet when we asked him why he would not say.

GERTRUDE
Did you suggest alternate therapy?

ROSENCRANTZ
As it happens, some players did show up,
And Hamlet smiled and was almost himself.[103]

104 *He is not convinced. But he wants to keep an eye on Hamlet.*
     And what could go wrong at a play performance?

105 *This is the king's first direct, confessional address to the*
     audience. His conscience troubles him. It does not, however,
     change his actions. Theologically this knowledge, and his
     resistance to genuine repentance, make him a doubly
     damnable sinner. Shakespeare will go on to stress the point. If
     vengeance is indeed the Lord's, Claudius will get it in spades.

POLONIUS

I can confirm that's my impression too.
Indeed, he did beseech me ask your majesties
To come and join him watch this evening's show.

CLAUDIUS

'Tis good to hear he might be on the mend.[104]

Exeunt Rosencrantz and Guildenstern

CLAUDIUS

And you must leave us too, my sweet Gertrude.
We've secretly arranged that Ham drops by
So that he chance upon Ophelia.
Then we might judge if his annoying angst
Is but the act of a young man in love.

Exit Gertrude

CLAUDIUS (*aside*)

We keep our fingers crossed it may be so,
The madness is just part of love's young dream.
For if he hath got whiff I killed his dad,
Things could get ugly for my conscience.
The harlot's cheek, betide with plastering art,
Is not more ugly to the thing that helps it
Than is my deed to my most painted word.[105]

106 This is one of the directorial cruxes in the play. Are the
     two main villains eavesdropping on Hamlet? Some critics
     suggest that he is aware of their presence, and that Hamlet
     is going into this meditation as a cunning act to throw his
     enemy off track.

107 It's English literature's most famous speech, in a play stuffed
     full of quotable quotes. However, Hamlet is not displaying
     high-powered original thought. 'To be or not to be' is a
     standard philosophy essay question. What we have here is
     not Hamlet the great thinker but Hamlet the undergrad.
     Some have difficulty with the seemingly ludicrous image of
     taking arms 'against a sea of troubles'. The allusion is to the
     Persian King Xerxes, who whipped the Hellespont when a
     storm destroyed his bridge. 'Conscience does make cowards
     of us all.' Of Hamlet, perhaps, but not Claudius. Hamlet is
     dangerously underestimating his 'mighty opposite', as he
     calls the king.

108 By Polonius's instruction, Ophelia is carrying a prayer book.
     That is why, later in the scene, after Hamlet has realised he
     is being spied on, he goes into his rant about 'nunneries', etc.
     Throughout the scene, Ophelia is careful to address Hamlet
     as 'my lord', stressing the social division between them.

POLONIUS

I hear him coming. Let's withdraw, my lord.

Exeunt Claudius and Polonius[106]
Enter Hamlet

HAMLET

To be, or not to be: that is the question,
The very essence of philosophy.
Whether 'tis nobler in the mind to suffer
The slings and arrows of outrageous fortune,
Or to take arms against a sea of troubles,
And by opposing end them. To die, to sleep;
To sleep, perchance to dream. Ay, there's the rub;
For in that sleep of death what dreams may come,
When we have shuffled off this mortal coil?
Or could it be that I o'er think my life
And take my torment far too personally?
From too much thought doth little action come,
Thus conscience does make cowards of us all.
So man up, Hamlet; get thyself stuck in.
Remember this: I think, therefore I am.[107]

OPHELIA

How does your honour for this many a day?[108]

HAMLET

Well, well, I thank you, lady; three times well.
Where is your father?

109 There is the by now familiar clock and calendar problem
again. Hamlet came back four months ago (at a generous
estimate), on his father's death. His thoughts would not
lightly turn to love. How do we make sense of the fact that
the affair with Ophelia seems to have been going on for
ages with letters and gifts? Ophelia says she has 'longed
long' to return them. The double time-scheme again.
Unless, that is, we assume the letters and gifts have come
from Wittenberg. But in the earlier exchanges between
Laertes and Polonius, it seems clear that the affair between
the prince and the only eligible woman in the court
(apparently) is a recent development.

110 Either he is trying to save her by making her hate him, or,
more likely, he's aware he's being watched and thinks she
is part of the conspiracy against him – she's the king's cat's
paw, like everyone in Elsinore except Horatio. Who has
temporarily disappeared.

OPHELIA

I'm not sure.
Here are some trinkets that you did give me.

HAMLET

Thou dost mistake me for a man who cares.

OPHELIA

It seems thy memory is playing up.
For thou didst hand me countless billets doux
That I no longer want and do return.[109]

HAMLET

Are you a virgin?

OPHELIA

What's it to you?

HAMLET

Oh, I dunno. I was just wondering. I did love
you once.

OPHELIA

So you said.

HAMLET

You didn't believe me, did you? I was only
joking. I never loved you.[110]

111   'Nunnery' was, we're told, street (and undergraduate) slang for 'brothel'. Hamlet begins this exchange by being polite to Ophelia and addressing her as 'Nymph', but at some point, we are to suspect, he realises that he is being watched. And that she is being pimped out.

112   He's playing savagely around the fact that she has a prayer book in her hand. And he continues to harp on the double meaning of 'nunnery'. It could be seen to suggest sexual relations between them. Or he could be trying to get her to come clean that she is conspiring against him.

113   Hamlet is not, as she now thinks, mad. He ends this scene with a direct threat to the listening Claudius's life. Soon poor Ophelia will know what true madness is.

OPHELIA

Then you deceived me.

HAMLET

Nymph, in thy orisons be all my sins remembered.
You've got a prayer book, so pray for me. In fact, why
don't you just have done with it and go to a nunnery?
After all, if you'd had kids with me they'd probably all
have been as nasty as me. I'm not a nice bloke at all.[111]

OPHELIA

What's the matter with you?

HAMLET

To be honest, your beauty has always been a bit over-
rated round here. You're got a funny walk, you've got
a lisp, and to cap it all, you're not that bright. Women
are such a handful. God hath given you one face and
you paint another. Like I said, go to a nunnery. It's the
best place for you.[112]

Exit Hamlet

OPHELIA

O how his mind unbalanced hath become,
My Hamlet's not the man that he once was.[113]
What have I done for him to betray love?
Without his love, life is not worth living.

Enter Claudius and Polonius

114   Claudius wants Hamlet to be killed outside the country
       (killing two Hamlets in the space of five months might not
       go down well with the Danish people). And he can blame
       perfidious Albion. Claudius is ever the arch-political criminal.
       England owes him a favour – they have not paid tribute –
       that is, fees for passage past Elsinore's coast. Claudius can
       call in that debt to have Prince Hamlet assassinated. In
       other circumstances, it would be an act of war. There is also
       the other problem, which is mentioned a couple of times
       in the action to come, that Hamlet (like his father) is very
       popular with the Danish people.

115   Polonius spends almost as much time behind the arras as in
       front of it. Gertrude's part in all this complicated interplay
       is not easy to work out. 'I will obey,' she tells Claudius. She
       has had, until this point, about a dozen words to say, and no
       revealing asides. The actress playing the part has to act with
       her face. A worried face. The one significant insight is her
       tenderness to Ophelia, who she hopes will marry Hamlet and
       bring him to his senses. Claudius has other plans.

CLAUDIUS

I do not see much sign of madness there,
There's surely more to this than meets the eye.
To England will I have the queen's son sent;
He cannot cause us trouble over there.[114]

POLONIUS

That sounds like it may be a decent plan,
Though first I'll eavesdrop on him and the queen,
To give her one last chance to find out why
Hamlet is being such a piece of work.[115]

Exeunt

116 At certain times in the play – during his encounter with the ghost, for example – Hamlet does display florid signs of hysteria. And it is only in that impulsive condition that he seems able to actually do anything. One of the interesting themes in this play is that you can think yourself into paralysis.

ACT 3, SCENE 2

The great hall of Elsinore castle

Enter Hamlet and the players

HAMLET
So here's how I want the play performed. Keep it natural. No over-blown speeches or over-acting. None of the method nonsense.[116]

PLAYER 1
You're a fine one to talk.

Exeunt players
Enter Horatio

HORATIO
Here, sweet lord, at your service.

HAMLET
Horatio, thou art a man I trust;
Seldom dost thou descend to flattery.
Remember what the ghost did say to me
About my father's untimely demise?

117 Horatio, the stoic, is a reliable observer. He is also stoically
     impassive. Hamlet does not trust himself. One must recall
     that Horatio doesn't seem to know all the details which the
     ghost divulged: that Claudius is a murderer. His witness of
     Claudius at the play will be wholly objective and unbiased.
     Hamlet, as the scene later shows, has the queen between
     himself and Claudius, obscuring his chance to see the king's
     features in what will unfold. This is the last test to see
     whether the ghost is a 'devil', or 'honest'.

118 Claudius pointedly does not say 'son'.

I beg thee then observe my uncle's face
During the play that soon will be performed.
And if thou thinks he shows sign of his guilt
Scratch your left ear and thus tip me the wink.[117]

HORATIO
That will I do, thou canst depend on me.

Enter Claudius, Gertrude, Polonius, Ophelia,
Rosencrantz and Guildenstern

CLAUDIUS
How are you, cousin Hamlet?[118]

HAMLET
Did someone say something?

GERTRUDE
Come and sit next to me, Hammy dear.

HAMLET
If it's all the same, I'll pass. You're not looking your
best today. But I could sit on Ophelia's lap.

OPHELIA
In your dreams. Don't be so smutty.

119 There is much bawdiness in this play – particularly in the opening exchanges with Hamlet's college pals, R&G. 'Country matters' is usually regarded as the most extreme example. Hamlet wants to shock. He is, unwittingly, driving poor Ophelia to distraction. And humiliating her in front of the whole court. She, of course, will be quite as smutty in her final mad scene, when her mind breaks.

120 Dumbshows served the same purpose as film trailers. They gave the audience some sense of where the action was going, what kind of play they could expect. This dumbshow has been concocted by Hamlet.

121 The king will know it is not coincidental. Moreover, he will know that the dumbshow will stir suspicion and gossip. He will be enthroned, centrally, and his face will be a study – not merely to Horatio.

122 The stylistic artificiality of The Murder of Gonzago has perplexed commentators because it runs so directly against the naturalistic (mirror-held-up-to-nature) instructions Hamlet gives the players. Nor is it clear which additional material Hamlet has inserted, except for details like 'thirty years' (the length of Old Hamlet's marriage to Gertrude). This is a scene which is often cut in modern productions of this extraordinarily long play.

HAMLET

   Did you think I meant country matters?[119] I was
   only trying to cheer myself up. How would you feel
   if your mum had remarried only two months after
   your dad died?

*A dumbshow begins. A king and queen embrace lovingly.
The king then lies down in some flowers and the queen
leaves. Another man comes in and tips poison in the king's
ear. The king croaks. The queen returns and gets in a bit of
a state, but then calms down and marries the poisoner.*[120]

OPHELIA

   What means this, my lord?

HAMLET

   It's just a bit of fun before the play begins.[121]

Enter Player King and Player Queen

PLAYER KING

   Full thirty summers have we both been wed,
   And ne'er an argument I can recall.[122]

PLAYER QUEEN

   To me it feels more like thirty winters,
   Though that may be just a minor detail.
   Still I confess thy health is some concern;
   Off-colour thou hast lately seemed to me.

123   It is clear that Hamlet is testing not just Claudius, but his mother as well. We may assume that if Horatio is studying Claudius's face from a decent distance, Hamlet is studying Gertrude's, who is alongside him.

124   'I know all' is the message Hamlet is getting across. But he does not know, or does not want to know (1) how complicit Gertrude was in the murder, if at all, and (2) what her earlier relationship with Claudius was. Deep waters. It is left to the discretion of the director and actress to reveal how guilty Gertrude is.

125   Gertrude, a woman of few words, does not admire female eloquence. This line is ambiguous: (1) 'The play is unconvincing,' (2) 'I'm beginning to feel very uncomfortable,' (3) 'Women should do what they're told and keep their mouths shut.'

126   The remark is also directed at Polonius. Danish drama (like Shakespeare's) needed to be passed for performance by a censor – the Lord Chamberlain. Polonius, we assume, has that role at Elsinore. It's clear that all he has done is look at the posters, otherwise he would never have allowed the play, clearly seditious, to be performed.

127   Elizabethan mousetraps, to venture a pedantic note, were much the same as ours. Elizabethans tended to have more household mice than us, of course. There were two kinds of trap: one was the spring and striker, breaking the vermin's back or trapping it; the other was a vessel which lured the mouse in, then released a closing panel behind it. Cat food on the way. There are a number of references in the play to rodents (four-legged and two-legged) behind the arras.

PLAYER KING

    'Tis true I am not feeling all that well,
    There is a chance that I may croak quite soon.

PLAYER QUEEN

    Well if thou dost, I will not wed again,
    For if I do I surely will be cursed.[123]

PLAYER KING

    Thou might full well believe thou speakest true,
    But once I'm gone, you'll surely change your mind.
    Give it two months or so, and thou wilt think
    A second marriage is a good idea.[124]
    Now I am tired and I need a kip,
    Pray leave me in this orchard for a snooze.

Exit Player Queen

HAMLET

    What do you think of it so far, Madam?

GERTRUDE

    The lady doth protest too much, methinks.[125]

CLAUDIUS

    What's this play called?[126]

HAMLET

    The Mousetrap.[127]

128 *Claudius is not necessarily admitting to any crime by*
     leaving so abruptly. His loyal courtiers (there are no other)
     will think that he considers Hamlet's choice of play, about
     regicide, offensive (Shakespeare's Richard II, *in which a*
     king is assassinated, had problems with the censors). It is
     typical of Hamlet to make his j'accuse *to the king through*
     literature. The poison in the ear – which only Hamlet Senior,
     Hamlet Junior and the poisoner, Claudius, know about – is
     the clincher. Hamlet knows not merely that Claudius is a
     murderer, but how he did it.

CLAUDIUS

It'll never catch on.

HAMLET

I wouldn't bet on it. It will pack out the West End for fifty years and counting.

Enter Player as Lucianus

HAMLET

This is Lucianus, nephew to the king.

OPHELIA

Are you going to keep up a running commentary throughout the play?

LUCIANUS

See here I have foul poison in my hands
That can extinguish life immediately.

Pours the poison in the king's ear

HAMLET

He's poisoning the king so he can marry the queen.

CLAUDIUS

I've had enough of this. Turn on the lights. I'm off.[128]

Exeunt all but Hamlet and Horatio

129   *Hamlet now has no reason to delay. But delay he does. What is stopping him?*

130   *Hamlet perceives that Gertrude, like Ophelia earlier, is acting on the instructions of Claudius and Polonius.*

HAMLET

Well, that went down a storm, didn't it? What do you reckon?

HORATIO

He acted guilty to me.

HAMLET

That's what I thought. The ghost called it right.[129]

Enter Rosencrantz and Guildenstern

GUILDENSTERN

The king isn't feeling at all well.

HAMLET

Maybe he's pissed.

GUILDENSTERN

No, he's just pissed off. But anyway, the queen bade us come to you.

HAMLET

And here I am.

ROSENCRANTZ

I can see that. He meant the queen wants a word with you in private about your behaviour.[130]

131 *He is testing to see how pliable Polonius is. Like putty,*
     he discovers.

HAMLET

I'm surprised she's noticed.

ROSENCRANTZ

Why are you being like this with us? We used to
be friends.

HAMLET

You can go off people. You're both treating me like a
half-wit. I won't be a pawn in someone else's game.

Enter Polonius

POLONIUS

The queen wants to speak to you right now.

HAMLET

Do you think that cloud looks like a cockapoo?[131]

POLONIUS

Since you mention it, I think it does.

HAMLET

Now there's a half-wit. Tell my mother I'll be along
in a while.

Exeunt all but Hamlet

132   *The scene which follows – with his mother, alone (less Polonius hiding) in her bedroom – is that on which the psychoanalytic theories have centred. They were formulated most articulately not by Freud himself (although he was intensely interested in the play), but by his British disciple, Ernest Jones. The way it goes is this. The Oedipus Complex (it could just as well be called the Hamlet Complex) is the first major psychic crisis a male child has to deal with, as his sexual desires emerge. The complex arises from two drives: (1) to kill his father, thereby (2) enabling him to sleep with his mother (raping her, if need be). Coming to terms with these two desires, by repression or sublimation (i.e. channelling their energy to more fruitful ends), creates the necessary step towards maturity and civilised behaviour. Call it self-control. The argument is that Hamlet has the dreaded 'unresolved Oedipal complex': because Claudius has reproduced his early-life crisis by killing his father and marrying his mother, Hamlet is paralysed.*

Nero, legend has it, enjoyed sexual relations with his mother, Agrippina. 'Let me be cruel, not unnatural,' says Hamlet – a remark which lends support to the Freudian reading that the following scene is highly sexually charged. And one can speculate that Hamlet is on his way to the bedroom in which he was conceived. Heady stuff.

HAMLET

'Tis now the very witching time of night
When churchyards yawn and hell itself breathes out
Contagion to this world. Soft! To my mother;
Though my incestuous urge I must resist,
'Tis not the time to be unnatural:
O heart, lose not thy nature; let not ever
The soul of Nero enter this firm bosom.
I will speak daggers to her, but use none.
In my revenge, I will leave her alive.

Exit[132]

133   Why not send him back to Wittenberg? Because, as
      mentioned in note 114, Claudius has relations with England
      that will enable him to dispose of his pesky nephew. No
      finals for student Hamlet.

134   They are Germans no more, but faithful Danskers. How
      much, though, have they worked out?

ACT 3, SCENE 3

The king's private chapel

Enter Claudius, Rosencrantz and Guildenstern

CLAUDIUS
Whether or no Hamlet is really mad,
I like him not. Therefore I you command
To England take him hence, out of my way.[133]

ROSENCRANTZ
That will we do, O wise and noble king!
Our one desire's to keep your highness safe.

Exit Rosencrantz and Guildenstern[134]
Enter Polonius

POLONIUS
Hot news I bring! Hamlet is on his way
Unto his mother's closet as we speak.
I'll take my place behind the queen's arras
And on their conversation report back.

Exit Polonius

135   *A politician to the core, Claudius thinks he can make a deal with God for having committed the mortal sin of Cain (and meanwhile laying plans to kill Hamlet). The king of heaven will be indulgent to the king of Denmark, surely? This is the first time Claudius levels with the audience, to whom this speech is directed.*

136   *Poor reasoning theologically. Cain was never forgiven. Hamlet is generally thought to be procrastinating here – he's lost his nerve.*

137   *Oh, the irony. Hamlet, had he been able to do the deed, would have been quite safe as regards the eternal damnation of Claudius's immortal soul. His chances are getting slimmer by the minute. From this moment onwards, Claudius quashes any remorse he may feel and sets himself the task of killing Hamlet. The great game between the two 'mighty opposites' has begun. The odds are in Claudius's favour.*

CLAUDIUS

    Oh my offence is rank, it smells to heaven;
    My guilt pours out of every orifice.
    What was I thinking when I killed my bro?
    For though I may have got to be the king,
    And had the queen as icing on the cake,
    But never can I enjoy peace of mind.
    Were I to pray from now to end of time,
    The gates of heaven would be closed to me.
    Yet as there's not much else that I can do,
    So will I kneel and ask to be forgiv'n.

He kneels[135]
Enter Hamlet

HAMLET

    'Tis just my luck that Claud is on his knees!
    If I do take him out while he doth pray,
    There's the odd chance he will to heaven go.
    I'll bide my time until the king be pissed
    And passed out in the queen's incestuous bed.
    Then he will not be spared, and go to hell.[136]

Exit Hamlet

CLAUDIUS

    This praying game is proving out of reach.
    My words fly up, my thoughts remain below;
    Words without thoughts never to heaven go.[137]

Exit Claudius

138 *Interesting that it is not the bedroom she shares with Claudius, but her private quarters. Directors are in two minds about whether there should be a bed in the room – but since a sheet is later needed, they routinely place one there.*

139 *The word 'father' will not help her maternal corrections. It would be interesting to know what conversation the king and queen had after the play within the play.*

140 *I.e. Old Hamlet. But the offence is not yet specified.*

141 *Like Claudius, Gertrude knows how to move from parental to regal as the moment requires. But Hamlet now is the loosest of cannons.*

ACT 3, SCENE 4

Gertrude's private room [138]

Enter Gertrude and Polonius

POLONIUS
Tell your Hamlet his attitude doth stink;
Give him both barrels, be not soft on him.

Polonius hides behind arras
Enter Hamlet

HAMLET
Yo, Mum. What's up?

GERTRUDE
Hamlet, thou hast thy father much offended. [139]

HAMLET
That's odd. I thought it was you who had offended
my father. [140]

GERTRUDE
I am the queen, speak not so cheekily. [141]

142 Polonius's hearing may be less than perfect. He merely hears
     some kind of threat involving slit throats.

143 Hamlet has drawn one of his weapons – a sword and
     dagger. Only nobles were permitted to carry them. Hamlet
     stabs the terrified Polonius through the arras under the
     misapprehension that he is killing the king. 'Dead for a
     ducat' is (1) what a rat-catcher would charge for clearing a
     house of vermin; (2) what someone laying a bet would say –
     i.e. 'I've stabbed him, and I bet he's dead. Anyone accept my
     bet for a ducat?' (All the bastard Claudius's life is worth.)

144 Hamlet's blood is up. Killing Polonius was merely a time out.
     Back to the real business – tearing his mother to pieces.

145 The accusation direct. Later in the scene, Hamlet swings
     round to the view that his mother was not complicit in her
     husband's killing; she, like him, was duped.

HAMLET

I know thou art the queen, and wish thou weren't;
For then thou would'st not sleep with Uncle Claud.
On this matter I will not hold my tongue,
Thy lack of shame is an embarrassment.

GERTRUDE

Dost thou intend to slit the royal throat?
Help, help![142]

POLONIUS (*from behind*)

Help, help!

HAMLET (*draws sword*)

How now! A rat? Dead, for a ducat, dead![143]

Strikes Polonius

POLONIUS (*from behind*)

It was an arras, not a rat. I'm slain!

GERTRUDE

Oh, what a rash and bloody deed is this![144]

HAMLET

'Tis not so bad, good mother, as killing
Thy husband and marrying his brother.

GERTRUDE

As kill a king?[145]

146 *Oddly, Gertrude does not contradict what looks like an*
     accusation of complicity against her. Guilt? Critics are divided.

147 *The Freudian thesis – that sexual envy is driving Hamlet –*
     is persuasive at this point.

HAMLET

Yes, you heard what I said.[146]

Pulls back arras and reveals body of Polonius

HAMLET

'Tis only the old fool that I have killed;
At least we are now spared him droning on.
And you can stop your crocodile sobbing,
'Tis for thy damnèd soul that thou should'st weep.
For thou dost shame the honour of true love.

GERTRUDE

What have I done that causes thee such pain?[147]

HAMLET

Add to thy many defects, being thick;
I do not see how I can plainer be.
But since thou asks, I will say it once more:
My father was a good and honest man,
Yet within fifty days of his demise
Thou didst have leg-over with evil Claud.

GERTRUDE

These words like daggers enter in my ears.

Enter ghost

HAMLET

Ah, look who has arrived!

148 The family reunited. Well, perhaps not. The ghost is wholly invisible to Gertrude, who now assumes that her son really has flipped his lid. The ghost could be a hallucinatory embodiment of Hamlet's conscience, telling him to get on with the job in hand and avenge his father. Old Hamlet is having a remarkably long basting in purgatory, one notes.

149 Possibly Old Hamlet is worried about his son doing a Nero on Gertrude.

150 They wholly ignore Polonius – whom rapid medical attention could perhaps save.

151 Hamlet assumes that his mother and stepfather are cohabiting vigorously. She does not contradict him. Nor, afterwards, does she tell Claudius what is now clear: that Hamlet's 'antic disposition' is not genuine but done 'in craft'. For what, Gertrude at this point dare not bring herself to think. One of the things that emerges from this scene, with all its 'bed' associations, is that the 'hey-day' in Gertrude's blood is not tame. She is still erotic, sexual, sensual.

GERTRUDE

He really is bonkers.[148]

GHOST

Do not thy mother give such a hard time,
My brother is the villain of the piece.[149]

GERTRUDE

Why dost thou stare intently into space?

HAMLET

Could you not see my father standing there,
As clear as day, before our very selves?

GERTRUDE

I beg you, Hamlet, do not be this way;
Thou needest help, I will get you a shrink.[150]

HAMLET

There's nothing wrong with me, of that I'm sure;
'Tis thee who dost need comfort for the soul.
Repent you of your deeds, I beg you, please!
As a first step, renounce your marriage bed;
Curbing your lust will help you get to heav'n.
Now one last favour do I ask of thee:
I beg you not to tell the king I'm sane.
If he gets wind of my plans for revenge,
I'll break thy pretty neck as well as his.[151]

152　*He takes away the evidence of his crime – not to hide it, but as a courtesy to his mother. In one of the main sources for the play, Saxo Grammaticus, he chops up Polonius's body and feeds it to the pigs. For this play, behind the arras on the stairs will suffice. Like Old Hamlet, Polonius has died without the offices of final unction. He and Old Hamlet will be able to chat about Denmark in purgatory.*

GERTRUDE
  This I can promise. I do want to live.

HAMLET
  First with Rosencrantz and Guildenstern
  I must board ship and sail towards England.
  But on the way, if they were both to slip
  Into the sea, then I could come straight back.
  So will I pack a rucksack, nothing more,
  Once I have lugged Pol's body from the room.

  Exit Hamlet, tugging Polonius in a sheet[152]
  Gertrude remains

153 It's heartless that she does not think of the effect on Ophelia
     – towards whom her feelings have been hinted to be tender.
     All the Polonius family are, suddenly, 'little people'.

154 Polonius, who thought himself so important, was never
     anything other than a court functionary for Claudius –
     someone to use, not respect or honour. Or even reward,
     substantially. But in not publicising the fact that 'mad'
     Hamlet has murdered a high court official, Claudius is making
     a serious political error. It will be assumed in the world
     outside (and, most dangerously, by Laertes) that Claudius
     was somehow involved. Or, at the very least, that he gave his
     'son and heir' carte blanche to do such things. By neglecting
     to publicise what Hamlet has done (perhaps to protect
     Gertrude's feelings), he imperils his hold on the throne.

ACT 4, SCENE 1

Gertrude's private room

Enter Claudius

CLAUDIUS
　What, Gertrude? How does Hamlet?

GERTRUDE
　Truth be known, as mad as any hatter;
　With his rapier, Hamlet hath killed
　That harmless old dullard, Polonius.[153]

CLAUDIUS
　That's not good news, it could well have been us;
　While Hamlet is still here, we are not safe.
　So, much as I do love thy noble son,
　'Tis better were he not to hang around.

Enter Rosencrantz and Guildenstern

CLAUDIUS
　I beg you, friends, remove the old man's corpse
　That Hamlet hath dragged out into the hall,
　And take it to the chapel, there to rest,
　So that Laertes can say his goodbyes.[154]

Exeunt

ACT 4, SCENE 2

A corridor in the castle

Enter Hamlet

HAMLET
Look who's coming. Denmark's very own Dumb
and Dumber.

Enter Rosencrantz and Guildenstern

ROSENCRANTZ
Where's the body?

HAMLET
What body?

ROSENCRANTZ
The dead one. The king wants it taken to the chapel.

HAMLET
You'll believe anything the king tells you.

155 *Hamlet hints to R&G that he's thrown the body in the sea so the old man can sleep with the fishes. And, who knows, Claudius may have fish for supper. In fact, he's hidden the corpse on a staircase, behind an arras – he loves arrases. Hamlet has gone to the trouble of removing the body so that Gertrude will not be thought guilty of being a party to the murder.*

ROSENCRANTZ
I'm not following you.

HAMLET
That rather proves my point.[155]

Exeunt

156 Claudius's hold on the throne is precarious. The Danish
people have not been mollified by his proclaiming Hamlet
next in line. And he's been distracted from making the
kind of royal progress (staying in grand houses around the
realm) that enabled monarchs of the period to ingratiate
themselves with the aristocracy and the masses.

ACT 4, SCENE 3

A state room

Enter Claudius

CLAUDIUS
   These are bad times with Hamlet on the loose,
   For he is much more popular than I.
   The throne is not secure with him around;
   I will not rest till in concrete he sleeps.[156]

Enter Rosencrantz

ROSENCRANTZ
   Ham will not tell us where the stiff be hid.

CLAUDIUS
   Then bring him before us to spill the beans.

Enter Hamlet and Guildenstern

CLAUDIUS
   So where's Polonius?

HAMLET
   With the maggots.

157 *England, as has been said, owes Denmark for some transgression – probably to do with trade routes – and there has been violence. Claudius is calling in the debt. What is interesting is Hamlet's passivity. Just as he meekly accepted the prohibition on going back to Wittenberg, he accepts exile to England. From there, he will not be able to carry out his revenge duties to the ghost. What plan, if any, does he have?*

CLAUDIUS

Stop messing about. Where is he?

HAMLET

Either in heaven or hell; your guess is as good as
mine. But if it's the latter, you can go and look for him
yourself. Judging by the smell, though, he's on the stairs.

CLAUDIUS

Since thou hast topped dear old Polonius,
I cannot guarantee to keep thee safe
Within the borders of these castle walls.
Hence I have fixed for you to take a ship
And sail tonight for England's dismal shores.

HAMLET

Great. Couldn't be better. I've always wanted to go
to England. Bye, Mum!

Exit Hamlet

CLAUDIUS

I bid you both, make sure he boards the boat,
He must away from Elsinore post-haste.[157]

Exeunt Rosencrantz and Guildenstern

CLAUDIUS

And when you read the letter I have writ,
In England shall the prince be murdered.

Exit

158　This is generally regarded as one of the more cuttable scenes in this long play – although film adaptors of Hamlet like it. It would have more life to it if the two princes met. They never do, although in the last scene Fortinbras behaves as if he knew Hamlet personally.

159　Given the fact that Fortinbras is lusting to revenge his father, we may suspect it's not merely logistical convenience that is on his mind.

160　It will be a long march. More likely it is the much-fought-over Baltic states that are ostensibly in Fortinbras's sights. Norway is in an expansive phase. Denmark is more quiescent – but Claudius is the better politician. The king of Norway, we are told, is frail and ineffective. Fortinbras is, effectively, in power.

ACT 4, SCENE 4

The sea coast near Elsinore[158]

Enter Fortinbras, the captain and an army

FORTINBRAS
Go, my captain, beseech the Danish king
That through his pleasant lands our men may march.[159]

Exit Fortinbras and army
Enter Hamlet

HAMLET
Who are you lot?

CAPTAIN
The Norwegians.

HAMLET
And where are you off to?

CAPTAIN
My lord, we are en route to some remote
Part of Poland that no one really wants.[160]

161 *So he thinks, as he goes off to England. Where, in all likelihood, he will do nothing except perhaps pop off to Oxford and read some of the wonderful books they have there. We have to assume that Hamlet is a man of languages: German and Latin in Wittenberg, Danish in Elsinore, and English in England.*

HAMLET

    I empathise with thy futility;
    For nothing gained, will many lives be lost.

Exit captain

HAMLET

    For too long hath my revenge been delayed;
    Procrastination be the death of me!
    See with what purpose the Norwegians move,
    E'en though there is no reason to make war,
    While I do have much honour in revenge
    And yet do naught but sit around and think.
    'Tis right for me to stop being so wet;
    Get off thy butt, Hamlet! From this time forth,
    My thoughts be bloody, or be nothing worth.[16]

Exit

162 What is Gertrude feeling guilty about? Plausibly it's her
     part in Polonius's death (she knew he was behind the arras,
     and it was her scream that led Hamlet to skewer him) and
     her failure to draw attention to his obscure burial, and
     she is too overcome to see how distraught Ophelia is. Who
     has been looking after Ophelia? She comes in unattended.
     Hamlet, of course, has not taken his leave from her.

163 It's the 'prologue to some great amiss', she says: a fine
     phrase. This is an aside, addressed to the audience. No other
     play of Shakespeare's creates a greater sense of intimacy
     between the auditorium and the stage.

ACT 4, SCENE 5

The great hall of Elsinore castle

Enter Gertrude and a gentleman

GERTRUDE
I will not speak with her.[162]

GENTLEMAN
I beg you, Madam, reconsider please,
Ophelia is with her dad obsessed,
And by her speech, one easily might think
That, like your son, she is not quite all there.

GERTRUDE
Let her come in.

Exit gentleman

GERTRUDE
About this I do have a bad feeling;
Conscience is not as clean as I would wish.
Strange noises I do hear within my head,
The sound of chickens coming home to roost.[163]

164 *Obviously, since the beauteous queen is standing in front of
     her, she is either out of her mind or ambiguously referring
     to Claudius, who she may think is responsible for her
     father's death.*

165 *Ophelia is sluttish in this scene, which discomforts and
     perplexes the audience. There are several schools of thought
     about her sudden vulgarity – she's been such a good girl until
     this point. One is that she is merely reflecting the rottenness
     at the core of Elsinore. Another is that her relationship with
     Hamlet went all the way, before he abandoned her. Hamlet's
     conduct towards Ophelia satisfies nobody. A third thesis is
     that only in madness can she speak her mind. What's left of it.*

Enter Ophelia, distracted

OPHELIA

People, good day, where is the beauteous majesty
of Denmark?[164]

GERTRUDE

I'm here.

OPHELIA (*sings*)

Kumbaya, my lord,
My dad is dead.

Enter Claudius

CLAUDIUS

How are you, my girl?

OPHELIA

Not so bad, if you like that sort of thing. Though
not so well, if you don't.

(*sings*)

There was a maid
Who did get laid.
After masculine urgin'
She was no longer a virgin.[165]

CLAUDIUS

Steady on, old girl.

166 Her farewell is exclusively to the 'sweet ladies' (Gertrude and her female attendant). Ophelia is finished with men.

167 Claudius instructs Horatio, of all people, to follow her and keep an eye on her. Which, as later events reveal, he signally fails to do. This is a perplexing detail, since Horatio is not one of Claudius's men. Ophelia needs, of course, women to superintend her and keep her from self-harm.

168 There must have been a time lapse for all this to happen. Chronology is best ignored in this section of the play (it's only a few hours' sail to England with a fair wind, which means that Hamlet should by now be dead). Why the 'rabble', as Claudius calls them, have transferred their allegiance from Hamlet (who as far as they know is still available) to Laertes is not easy to account for. But the action is moving so fast at this stage that such complications are overlooked by the audience.

OPHELIA (*sings*)
> I feel so alone
> Now my man has gone,
> He's gone to the bad
> And I'm sad and mad.

CLAUDIUS
> How long hath she been thus?

OPHELIA
> Don't worry about me. I'll be OK. Or maybe I won't.
> Good night, sweet ladies.[166]

Exit Ophelia

CLAUDIUS
> Keep an eye on her, Horatio.[167]
> Gertrude, my love, I'm almost on my knees;
> When sorrows come, they always come in threes.
> The girl is understandably upset
> About her father's death and hath gone mad.
> Meanwhile her brother hath from France returned
> To find out what the hell is going on.
> And if that weren't enough trouble, today
> The Danish natives have become restless.

Enter a messenger

MESSENGER
> Laertes hath whipped up a goodly crowd,
> Some of whom think he should be Denmark's king.[168]

169 *An interesting introduction of the divine right of kings – the*
king of heaven protects them. Nonetheless, we are told that
Claudius's close-protection soldiers are Swiss mercenaries.
He does not trust Danish soldiers. It is significant that,
at this moment when his life is threatened, Claudius
shows courage. It raises in the audience's mind the awful
possibility that he may win, after all. They, of course, know
that Hamlet was supposedly sailing off to sudden death.

170 *She distributes wild flowers – some with bawdy names.*

Enter Laertes

LAERTES

    O vilest king, why is my father dead,
    And my dear sister lost unto the birds?

CLAUDIUS

    Calm down, young man! Why art thou mad at me?
    No wrong have I done you or anyone.
    Nor do I fear your fiery temper,
    For God always protects our royal blood,
    Except the time he forgot Hamlet's dad.[169]

LAERTES

    Talking of fathers, where's Polonius?

CLAUDIUS

    Try to distinguish between friend and foe,
    I swear on my own life I'm not to blame.
    While I do understand you want revenge,
    'Tis wise to take it on the guilty man.

Enter Ophelia[170]

LAERTES

    Heaven be cursed. Look at the state of her,
    She is clearly away with the fairies.

171   One of the things that most upsets Laertes is the fact
      that his father was buried without 'trophy, sword, nor
      hatchment'. There was no 'noble rite'. Claudius immediately
      sees his weak point – he wants social advancement. He can
      be flattered into usefulness, as was his father. And bribed.
      Laertes becomes Claudius's man as promptly and servilely as
      did his father.

172   And promotion. He's an easily bought man.

OPHELIA (*sings*)
Hey nonny, nonny,
My dad's not so bonny.

LAERTES
Her singing is rubbish and she's singing rubbish.

OPHELIA (*sings*)
Everyone is dead,
Or else has gone to bed.

Exit Ophelia

LAERTES
This is too much.[171]

CLAUDIUS
Weep not, my boy, for I do feel thy pain,
'Tis never easy when thy father's slain.
Yet know one thing, this will I promise thee:
If thou canst prove I killed Polonius,
Then will I make thee king instead of me.

LAERTES
In faith, a man cannot much fairer say;
I will seek out the truth and have revenge.[172]

Exeunt

ACT 4, SCENE 6

A room in the castle

Enter Horatio and an attendant

ATTENDANT
A seafaring man has given me this letter for you.

HORATIO
'Dear Horatio, please remember to read this letter out loud or the scene isn't going to work very well. Just to let you know my ship was seized by pirates. But don't worry, I'm OK, as I have done a deal with the pirates and am back home. I've sent a letter to the king, but it would be great to meet up with you ASAP. Lots of love, Hamlet.'

Exeunt

173   *This very long conspiratorial scene between Claudius and Laertes is generally regarded as somewhat redundant. Its purpose seems to be to allow the actor playing Hamlet time to refresh himself and rest for the excessively energetic demands to be made on him in the final scenes.*

174   *Superficially true: Hamlet destroyed Ophelia's reputation and killed Polonius. As ever with Claudius, it is what he cunningly withholds that matters.*

ACT 4, SCENE 7

A state room in the castle

Enter Claudius and Laertes[173]

CLAUDIUS

Now must your conscience my acquittal seal,
And me acknowledge to be friend and king,
Since you have heard from others you can trust
That Hamlet is the one whom you should blame.[174]

LAERTES

It well appears that you told me the truth,
Yet one thing doth still bother me a lot.
If thou didst know that Hamlet was guilty,
How come thou didst not do much about it?

CLAUDIUS

Dear Laertes, it is complicated;
Polonius was not the only one
Whom Hamlet had his beady eyes set on;
In his madness, which I have clean forgot,
He also rudely threatened to kill me.
Yet I did dare not punish him right then

175 *This is an interesting confidence. Claudius admits that he loves Gertrude so much that he cannot do what royal and state duty require. He cannot do anything that would upset her. He is probably lying. The real reason is that Young Hamlet has all the affection Old Hamlet accumulated in the thirty years of his reign. Claudius does not say that he has made firm arrangements for Hamlet to be dead by now (which would have been the most important confidence of all).*

Because the queen is very fond of him.
Also remember, although God knows why,
That Hamlet is beloved of all Danes,
And were he to be topped, they might top me.[175]

LAERTES
I take your point. But where does that leave me,
If my vengeful desires cannot be met?

CLAUDIUS
Break not your sleeps for that: you must not think
That we are made of stuff so flat and dull
That we can't think of something to please thee.

Enter a messenger with a letter

CLAUDIUS
How now? What news?

MESSENGER
Letters, my lord, from Hamlet.

Exit messenger

CLAUDIUS (*aside*)
How can this be? I thought the bastard dead.
– Let's see, Laertes, what Ham has to say.

'Your most high and mighty blah blah, as you can tell,
I am very much alive and well and back in Denmark.

176   Laertes knows nothing of the English plot. We, thanks to the other letter sent to Horatio, are privy to this twist. The 'pirates' episode is, of course, pure improbability. If they had rescued Hamlet, they would have wanted a sizeable ransom. Hamlet unconvincingly describes them as 'thieves of mercy'. One of the many mysteries is why Hamlet does not do what Laertes does: exploit his popularity with the Danish people and storm Elsinore. The ghost, wherever he is, must be suffering frustration worse than the pangs of purgatory.

177   This is the first we hear of Hamlet's pride in his fencing skill. It rather goes against the pronounced bookishness of his character, of which we have had plentiful evidence.

If a little chilly. Tomorrow I should like to swing by
and tell you what occurred. Hamlet.'

LAERTES

This sounds to me as if it be good news,
For now I'll get the chance for my revenge.[176]

CLAUDIUS

Why do these things keep happening to me?
I needs must think quite quickly on my feet.
I beg you this, Laertes: still your sword,
And only act when I give thee the word.

LAERTES

That do I give.

CLAUDIUS

Thou will not waiteth long,
But first let me digress a little while
And chunter on how Hamlet envies thee.
When thou were far away from court in France,
A Norman called Lamond did this way come,
And for thy swordsmanship was full of praise,
Such that Hamlet went red and did exclaim,
'He cannot surely be as good as me.'[177]

LAERTES

I like this tale, yet see not where it leads.

CLAUDIUS

Another thing that has been troubling me

178　They will be fencing with buttoned weapons and masks. Osric, the referee, will make sure that Laertes has the deadly rapier ('a sword unbated', without its protective button). Hamlet will pay for sneering at the young fellow. It's interesting that Laertes has acquired this 'deadly poison' (from a 'mountebank', he says). He clearly does not like to lose.

179　The drink, called by Claudius a 'union' (signifying togetherness) is for Hamlet if he happens to win. Each of the contestants would have their own chalice of refreshing water, or whatever.

Is the abstract nature of time's arrow.
For with each passing hour it doth seem
That man becomes distracted from his dreams.
So I do fear that thy hatred might wane,
Such that thou can't kill Hamlet in a fight.

LAERTES

Though this our conversation I've enjoyed,
It feels to me it hath gone on too long.

CLAUDIUS

Thou hast forgot the basics of stagecraft:
Hamlet doth need a break 'fore the last act.
But time enough to chill hath he now had,
No more delay, we can cut to the chase.
When Ham returns, challenge him to a duel,
And though his blade be blunted, yours be true,
So when the time is right, you run him through.

LAERTES

I like the sound of this, but to make sure,
My sword I'll dip in a deadly poison.[178]

CLAUDIUS

Too careful can the wise man never be,
Thus just in case Hamlet gets lucky breaks,
Into his drink, poison I'll also tip.
This triple jeopardy he can't survive.[179]

Enter Gertrude

180   *Ophelia was, in her madness, obsessed with wild flowers. But is Gertrude falsifying, with this beautiful speech? It's clear from the burial scene that Ophelia's death is judged to have been suicide, not accidental. And what was Horatio's role in all this? He was specifically charged to keep an eye on her. Did the letter from Hamlet and the need to conduct him back to Elsinore distract him? Some of the details Gertrude gives – that Ophelia was singing to the end – make it clear there were witnesses. Why did they not rescue her?*

181   *He will now show Hamlet how revenge should be carried out.*

GERTRUDE

    One woe doth tread upon another's heel,
    So fast they follow. Your sister's drowned, Laertes.

LAERTES

    Drowned! Oh where?

GERTRUDE

    There is a willow grows aslant a brook,
    That shows his hoar leaves in the glassy stream;
    There with fantastic garlands did she come,
    Until she stretched too far and did fall in.
    So heavy did her garments then become
    She was pulled under so she could not breathe.[180]

LAERTES

    Alas, then she is drowned?

GERTRUDE

    Hast thou not listened to a word I've said?
    Yes, she is drowned and lieth stone-cold dead.

LAERTES

    Too much of water hast thou, poor Ophelia,
    And therefore I must try to stem my tears.
    Let a bright fire burn within my soul.[181]

Exeunt

182   *We must assume some time has passed, sufficient for Claudius*
to have got dispensation from the Church for Ophelia to be
buried in its consecrated soil. The burial of suicides was a
grim business. Suicide was considered self-murder – a felony
– and its very nature meant that no final confession could be
made. It led to posthumous conviction by the coroner's court.
The body, and heirs, were punished. Property was confiscated.
Christian burial was forbidden. The corpse was buried at
a crossroads, face-down, naked, with a stake hammered
through the body. No ritual was allowed. There was occasional
dispensation for suicide non compos mentis *– while the*
balance of the mind was disturbed. Claudius has obviously
played that card. But the Church authorities have only
allowed a very reduced and bleak interment.

ACT 5, SCENE 1

A graveyard near the castle

Enter two gravediggers

FIRST GRAVEDIGGER
This Ophelia woman . . .

SECOND GRAVEDIGGER
What of her?

FIRST GRAVEDIGGER
How come she is going to get a proper Christian burial
when she topped herself?[182]

SECOND GRAVEDIGGER
'Cos the coroner said so. When a posh bird offs herself,
the rules change. So get digging. I'm outta here.

Exit second gravedigger
Enter Hamlet and Horatio

FIRST GRAVEDIGGER (*sings*)
Hey, ho! Hey, ho!

183 There were no municipal cemeteries, graveyards got crowded, and (particularly in times of plague) the same plots were used over and over. Yorick – a notable figure in the court, surely with a tombstone – is being displaced.

184 Shakespeare unwinds somewhat in this comic scene.

185 'Quick' meaning 'live' as well as 'quick-witted'. It may cross the audience's mind that Old Hamlet's body is in the graveyard too. It isn't – it's down the coast at Roskilde cathedral in Copenhagen, along with all the nation's kings (soon to include Claudius and Hamlet).

It's off to dig we go,
To turn the clods
And bury poor sods,
Hey ho! Hey ho! Hey ho! Hey ho!

He digs up a skull[183]

HAMLET
Who do you reckon that was, Horatio? A courtier?

HORATIO
Could have been, I suppose.

HAMLET
'Twas better had it been a lawyer. The world's got too
many of those shysters as it is. Tell me, sirrah, whose
grave is that?

FIRST GRAVEDIGGER
Since I'm digging it, it must be mine.[184]

HAMLET
Thou hast a quick wit, but a grave is not for the quick.
What man is it intended for?[185]

FIRST GRAVEDIGGER
It isn't.

HAMLET
Then what woman?

186 The gravedigger has picked up interesting factual details
from local gossip. He does not, of course, know that Hamlet
is returned. It's strange that he doesn't recognise him, smart
fellow that he is.

187 It was also thirty years ago that Old Hamlet was away
on the battlefield, killing Old Fortinbras. A busy year. Why
Shakespeare should have so deliberately introduced this fact
about Hamlet's age has perplexed critics.

188 An insight into the difference between Old Hamlet and
Claudius. Jesters are very old hat. (The octogenarian King Lear
has one.) Claudius – the diplomat king – would no more have
a jester than wear a cap and bells himself.

FIRST GRAVEDIGGER

An ex-woman.

HAMLET

You're almost as much hard work as me. How long have you been in the gravedigging racket?

FIRST GRAVEDIGGER

Since our last King Hamlet o'ercame Fortinbras.

HAMLET

And when was that?

FIRST GRAVEDIGGER

Thirty years ago. The very same day young Hamlet, who's since gone mad and been shipped off to England, was born.[186]

HAMLET

Then that must make me thirty.[187] Who would have guessed? By the way I've been behaving these past four hours, most people would have had me down for a teenager. Tell me, though. How long does it take for a corpse to rot?

FIRST GRAVEDIGGER

Depends on conditions. See this skull here? It's been here for twenty-three years. It's Yorick, the king's jester.[188]

189   *By this stage in the play Hamlet is entirely gynophobic,*
      suggesting to some modern commentators a love relationship
      with faithful Horatio.

190   *There is some confusion here. Since Horatio was dispatched*
      to look after Ophelia, he must know she's dead. But he has
      not informed Hamlet. Nor, apparently, has he told him that
      Laertes has returned with a mob in attendance (a fact not
      easily overlooked, since it puts the throne at risk). What, then,
      have Horatio and Hamlet been talking about? Aristotle?

191   *Nor, as Laertes complains, will the church walls display her*
      'virgin crants', indicating she died a pure maid.

HAMLET

Alas, poor Yorick! He looks not at all well.
I knew him, Horatio: a fellow of infinite jest,
Though sadly finite breath.
Though thy gibes be still, yet still thou grins;
I seldom saw thy teeth look quite so clean.
We're all going to end up like this one day, Horatio.
Kings, queens and princes: none can escape the grave.
Get you to my lady's bed-chamber, and tell her, let her
paint an inch thick, to this favour must she come. Make
her suck on that.[189]

Enter Claudius, Gertrude, Laertes and priest, with coffin

HAMLET

Who is this they follow? Such maimed rites
Must surely be a sign of suicide.

Retires with Horatio[190]

PRIEST

Her death was doubtful, but she was well-born,
And so we must accord her benefit
Of holy grave. Yet ceremony brief;
There is no more that I can do for her.[191]

LAERTES

How dare you be quite so perfunctory?
My sis is purer than you'll ever be.

192 An interesting revelation on Gertrude's part. But it is hard
     to see that it would have made political sense, if Hamlet
     were the heir apparent. 'Sweet', incidentally, at this period
     meant 'sweet-smelling', not 'sweet-tasting'. The great sugar
     importation had not yet started. Gertrude is throwing flowers,
     not jelly babies, into the grave.

193 That wild shout, 'This is I, Hamlet the Dane,' will have sent a
     chill through Claudius. It is another way of saying 'This is I,
     King of Denmark.' In the last few days, two young men have
     claimed his throne.

194 Two men brawling over a grave: over the very body of Ophelia,
     one deduces. One hopes that (in contravention of the rules for
     the bodies of suicides) she has a shroud, at least.

HAMLET
    Ophelia?

GERTRUDE (*scattering flowers*)
    Sweets to the sweet: farewell!
    I hoped thou should'st have been my Hamlet's wife.[192]

LAERTES
    Let curses fall upon that madman's head
    Whose vilest deeds led to her suicide.

                    Leaps into the grave

    Now pile your dust upon the quick and dead,
    Till of this flat a mountain you have made.

HAMLET (*advancing*)
    With thy grief thou makest too big a deal;
    I am the only one who loved her so.
    Get away. This is I, Hamlet the Dane.[1934]

    Laertes climbs out of the grave and grapples with him

HAMLET
    I prithee take thy fingers from my throat,
    For though I do not wish you any harm,
    I am mad, bad and dangerous to know.

                Laertes and Hamlet are parted[1945]

195　This, recall, is the same Hamlet who instructed the travelling actors not to overdo their performance, here mocking Laertes' hyperbole. He does not come out well from this scene, which gives credence to critics who see something of the lout in him.

GERTRUDE
  O my dear son, what art thou on about?

HAMLET
  I loved Ophelia: forty thousand brothers
  Could not, with all their quantity of love,
  Make up my sum. What wilt thou do for her?
  While thou dost little but keen howling make,
  It is my heart, my heart alone, that breaks.
  Whate'er thou says, I'll rant as well as thou.[195]

GERTRUDE
  It seems my son hath had another turn.
  Ignore his words: we'll talk when he calms down.

HAMLET
  Let Hercules himself do what he may,
  The cat will mew, the dog will have its day.

Exit Hamlet

CLAUDIUS (*to Laertes*)
  Remember what we spake of late last night;
  The time of your vengeance is almost nigh.

Exeunt

196 *It will also have crossed the audience's mind.*

ACT 5, SCENE 2

The great hall of Elsinore castle

Enter Hamlet and Horatio

HAMLET
You're prob'ly wondering how I got here,
When you last saw me get on to the ship.

HORATIO
Since now you bring it up, indeed I was,
Yet was much too polite to mention it.[196]

HAMLET
It was like this, my good Horatio.
One night I could not sleep in my cabin,
So ventured out on deck to get a snack,
And on the galley table I did see
The letter R and G had been given.
This I did open, and to my surprise,
They had been told to o'ersee my demise.
These orders did I change so that they read
'Twould be the deadly twins that wound up dead.

197   They 'did make love to this employment', says Hamlet. Their
      employment? Espionage. They did not, one assumes, know
      the contents of the correspondence they were carrying.
      Or perhaps they did, otherwise they might have sprung to
      Hamlet's defence when, on reading the letters, the English
      promptly attempted to slit his throat, if things had gone
      according to plan.

198   'Young Osric' could mean (1) Osric the Younger, or (2) a young
      man about court. The name is Anglo-Saxon in origin and is a
      noble Scandinavian name (there have been kings called Osric),
      and the detail is given us that his family is rich and noble.
      Hence his admissibility to the king's entourage.

199   Young Osric is chronically nervous about wearing his hat
      in the presence of a prince. A 'water fly' – or fairy – he is
      sometimes, in modern productions, played as gay. But then so
      is Hamlet sometimes. And Horatio.

HORATIO

    Didst thou not think that was a trifle harsh?

HAMLET

    Not for a second did I have a doubt,
    Good riddance to bad rubbish and all that.[197]
    Talking of which, I shall kill Claudius,
    He that hath killed my king and whored my ma,
    Though since I've had some time to give it thought,
    I have too hasty been with Laertes;
    'Tis not his fault that I did kill his dad.

HORATIO

    Good point, well made. Now, prithee, who comes here?

Enter young Osric[198]

OSRIC

    Welcome back to Denmark.

HAMLET

    Thank you. Do you know this bloke, Horatio?

HORATIO

    Never set eyes on him before in my life.

HAMLET

    Well, take it from me, he's a complete nobody. Tell me,
    nobody, what do you want? And put your bonnet back
    on. You'll catch your death.[199]

200 Osric stresses Laertes' breeding. The Polonius family is not high-born, as we have seen from the way in which its deceased members are disposed of. Hamlet is contemptuous.

201 In the Renaissance duel, the two-handed rapier-and-dagger contest was common, the dagger being used in the left hand, not to stab but to parry. In night-time duels, the left arm would sometimes be used to hold a lantern (the posture, without a lantern, survived – left arm behind the body above the head). The French were particularly noted for their duelling skill. Laertes, who has been trained in Paris, will be a formidable foe.

OSRIC

I'm fine, thanks. The thing is, the king has laid
a wager . . .

HAMLET

I'm all ears.

OSRIC

'Tis like this. There is this gentleman, Laertes, the
very card or calendar of the gentry . . .[200]

HAMLET

The very card or calendar of the gentry? Ooh, get you . . .
And?

OSRIC

Laertes is much accomplished with dagger and rapier.
So the king has bet that in a first-to-twelve duel,
Laertes will not win three bouts more than you.[201]

HAMLET

Sounds like fun. I'll win for him if I can. If not,
I'll lose.

Exit Osric

HORATIO

What a tosser!

202 One has to wonder what Hamlet's game is here. When precisely and how does he intend to settle his score with Claudius?

HAMLET
My thoughts exactly.

Enter a lord

LORD
Are you ready for the duel? The king and queen await.

Exit

HORATIO
You'll lose.

HAMLET
I'm as ready as I'll ever be.

Enter Claudius, Gertrude and Laertes
Hamlet takes Laertes by the hand

HAMLET
Give me your pardon, sir: I've done you wrong,
Your father I should not have run clean through,
Though in a sense I too am a victim
Of the wild madness that came over me.[202]

LAERTES
Don't push your luck too far, my noble prince,
Though thine apology I do accept.
Now let us choose our foils and rapiers
And get on with the business in hand.

203 With Fortinbras and a whole army lurking outside the castle walls, we may wonder what the ever-treacherous Claudius is up to. It is not too fanciful to suspect that he has arranged for what will be a mysterious death or two (in fact there will be four) to be interrupted by Fortinbras (we know there has been correspondence between them), so that, in the ensuing confusion, a very suspicious set of circumstances with many inconvenient witnesses can be glossed over. Or perhaps Shakespeare just wanted to get the bloody play over with.

204 Osric is referee. He is also clearly an expert fencer.

205 Claudius's agonised aside to the audience. Keeping up with events at this hectic stage of the play is not easy.

CLAUDIUS
    If Hamlet be the victor we shall drink
    And make the cannons ready for salute.[203]

They start duelling

OSRIC
    A hit, a very palpable hit. One–nil to Hamlet.[204]

CLAUDIUS
    'Tis thirsty work; Hamlet, have this to drink.

HAMLET
    Not now I won't; perhaps in a short while.

They duel again

LAERTES
    A touch, a touch, I do confess.

HAMLET
    Two–nil to me.

GERTRUDE
    Though thou aren't thirsty, I could use a drink.

She drinks

CLAUDIUS *(aside)*
    It is the poisoned cup. It is too late.[205]

206 Hamlet now has the unbuttoned weapon, and should evince surprise.

207 There are a number of hints in the duel scene that young Osric is in on the Claudius–Laertes plot.

208 A spring-operated trap is alluded to here. It reminds us that Shakespeare was a country boy who was perhaps once arrested for poaching in his wild young days. It may not be true, but it has a certain plausibility. One can picture the lad Will coming home with one or two illicit (and highly edible) woodcocks.

209 How on earth did Claudius think the mass poisonings taking place in full view of the gathered court would go unnoticed? The improbability quotient is pretty high here.

HAMLET

Come for the third, Laertes: you but dally;
See if you can do better this time round.

LAERTES

Have at you now!

Wounds Hamlet. In scuffling they exchange rapiers

HAMLET

Nay, come again.

Wounds Laertes [206]

OSRIC

How is't, Laertes? [207]

LAERTES

Why, as a woodcock to mine own spring, Osric; [208]
I am justly killed with mine own treachery.

Gertrude falls

GERTRUDE

No, no, the drink, the drink – O my dear Hamlet,
The drink, the drink! – I am poisoned.

Gertrude dies [209]

210 *This scene – one of the most challenging action scenes in Shakespeare – demands actors who can fence convincingly (and safely) and who can carry off this extremely tricky exchange of foils, mid-duel.*

211 *Dane = king of Denmark. But not for much longer. At long last, Hamlet acts. A scratch from an envenomed sword would take some time to kill – which is what Claudius wanted. If Hamlet died mid-contest, in public, from a poisoned foil, it would be too obvious. Logically there should also be a slow-acting poison in the potion. Hence the need for knives.*

212 *Of course they do. One of the things Shakespeare has to do in this revenge play is not to glorify revenge, which was sternly disapproved of in England.*

HAMLET
  Oh villainy! What villainy occurs!

Laertes falls

LAERTES
  It is here, Hamlet: Hamlet, thou art slain,
  For I did smite thee with a poisoned sword,
  And since we did swap blades in the mêlée
  'Tis certain that I am a goner too.[210]

HAMLET
  I'm not that bothered; venom, do thy worst!

Hamlet stabs the king

HAMLET
  Here, thou incestuous, murderous, damned Dane,
  Drink off this poison, get it down your throat.[211]

King dies

LAERTES
  No one can blame you, he was justly served,
  A nasty piece of work was Claudius.
  Exchange forgiveness with me, noble Ham:
  Mine and my father's death come not on thee.[212]

Laertes dies

213   *The improbably extended death-scene speech was a*
      commonplace of Jacobean tragedy, and often joked about.

214   *Just dropping by? Or has Claudius been negotiating with him*
      (as with the English) through back channels? The politics of
      the last scene is a bit fuzzy. It's inconceivable that Claudius,
      with his keen interest in intelligence, did not know that there
      was a foreign army on his borders. Or that a foreign army
      could simply march into Elsinore unresisted.

215   *Odd that the country should now pass to its sworn enemy.*
      But there is no obvious successor. And no commander.
      (Where, incidentally, have Denmark's armed forces been?) But
      historically, as Shakespeare well knew, Denmark–Norway (as
      the union was called at this period) was ruled by Christian
      IV of Norway, whose sister Anne married James I of England.
      When Shakespeare wrote Hamlet, *Christian was regarded*
      as an enlightened, modern monarch (with a Danish love of
      excessive drinking).

216   *'His' here could mean Claudius or Hamlet. One can't*
      (particularly if one's seen Stoppard's play, Rosencrantz and
      Guildenstern are Dead*) suppress a spasm of sympathy for R&G.*

HAMLET

> Though everyone has died from this poison,
> I can still walk and talk quite easily.
> For now we will o'erlook that plot fault-line
> And concentrate on ending this my play.
> Pass me that damnèd cup, Horatio,
> And when I die make sure the whole world knows
> I was a decent bloke for the most part.[213]

OSRIC

> Young Fortinbras with conquest comes from Poland.[214]

HAMLET

> No false alarm this time, I surely die,
> I promise these shall be my final words.
> Let Fortinbras elected be the king,
> So tell him, with the occurrents, more and less,
> Which have solicited. The rest is silence.

Hamlet dies[215]
Enter Fortinbras and English ambassador

FORTINBRAS

> Christ, what a mess! What has been going on
> That all these royals have been killed at once?

AMBASSADOR

> Dismal, indeed, and I suspect too late
> To tell him his commandment is fulfilled:
> That Rosencrantz and Guildenstern are dead.[216]

217 *'Denmark' is used in two significant ways in* Hamlet: *(1) as the country, (2) as the king. Horatio is here assuming that, very briefly, Hamlet was King Hamlet II, and that it was in his gift to hand the throne over to a foreigner.*

218 *Fortinbras's potentially redundant speech was in fact necessary. The Globe had no curtains. Getting four corpses (three of them royal, all of them breathing heavily) ceremonially off the stage was tricky. Hence the musical and ballistic accompaniment.*

HORATIO

Just one more thing Denmark doth ask of thee.
Norway is very drab; become our king.[217]
So let us raise these bodies on a bier,
Though don't forget that Hamlet's must be higher.
For of this show he surely is the star,
And would not want to share the curtain call.

FORTINBRAS

Gladly do I accept to be your king,
Offers like this do not arrive each day.
A state funeral is Hamlet's princely right.
Let cannons fire and trumpet fanfares sound.
Go, bid the soldiers shoot.[218]

Exeunt

John Crace is the *Guardian*'s parliamentary sketch writer and author of the 'Digested Read' column, and he writes regularly for *Grazia*. He is the author of *I Never Promised You a Rose Garden: A Short Guide to Modern Politics, the Coalition and the General Election* and also *Baby Alarm: A Neurotic's Guide to Fatherhood*; *Vertigo: One Football Fan's Fear of Success*; *Harry's Games: Inside the Mind of Harry Redknapp*; *Brideshead Abbreviated: The Digested Read of the Twentieth Century* and *The Digested Twenty-first Century*.

John Sutherland is Lord Northcliffe Professor Emeritus of Modern English Literature at University College London and previously taught at the California Institute of Technology. He writes regularly for the *Guardian* and *The Times* and is the author of many books, including *Curiosities of Literature*, *Henry V, War Criminal?* (with Cedric Watts), biographies of Walter Scott, Stephen Spender and the Victorian elephant Jumbo, and *The Boy Who Loved Books*, a memoir.

TRANSWORLD PUBLISHERS
61–63 Uxbridge Road, London W5 5SA
www.penguin.co.uk

Transworld is part of the Penguin Random House group of companies
whose addresses can be found at global.penguinrandomhouse.com

Penguin
Random House
UK

First published in Great Britain in 2016 by Doubleday
an imprint of Transworld Publishers

A CIP catalogue record for this book
is available from the British Library.

ISBN 9780857524287

Typeset in 11/13pt Berylium by Julia Lloyd Design.
Printed and bound by Clays Ltd, Bungay, Suffolk.

Penguin Random House is committed to a sustainable
future for our business, our readers and our planet. This book
is made from Forest Stewardship Council® certified paper.

1 3 5 7 9 10 8 6 4 2